# NOTTINGHAM'S
# NEW TRAMS

## THE NET SUCCESS

Geoffrey Skelsey

ISBN No: 978-0-948106-33-0

*Above: Nottingham's stylish new trams complement the city's fine buildings: shortly after the system opened in 2004 a southbound tram stands outside the Council House.*

*Cover: NET's branch to Phoenix Park follows the road bed of a former mineral railway, and some of its attractive nineteenth century bridges were reused. The twisting track beyond Cinderhill station resembles a rural branch line. On this section concrete slab trackbed is used.*

ISBN No: 978-0-948106-33-0

Written by Geoffrey Skelsey

Additional photography by Martin Cobley

Designed and Published by LRTA Publishing Ltd, PO Box 26, Sawtry PE28 5WY
E-mail: *editor@lrta.org*

Printed by Wyndeham Gait Ltd, Castle Press, Victoria Street, Grimsby DN31 1PY
E-mail: *gait@wyndeham.co.uk*

LRTA Publications, 7 Ramsdale Court, 31 Esplanade Gardens, Scarborough YO11 2AP
E-mail: *booksales@lrta.org*

**LRTA**

# NOTTINGHAM'S NEW TRAMS
## THE NET SUCCESS STORY

### Geoffrey Skelsey
Including additional photographs by Martin Cobley

## Contents

## Foreword

by the Rt Hon Lord Broers, ScD, FRS, FREng
Chairman of the House of Lords Select Committee on Science and Technology, Past President of the Royal Academy of Engineering, Emeritus Professor of Electrical Engineering in the University of Cambridge.

"Having been brought up in Melbourne I have always liked trams and thought of them as an ideal form of urban transportation. I recall it being a matter of pride to us in 1950s that the old Melbourne and Metropolitan Tramways Board were still building new trams (and indeed a new tram line) when most other Australian cities were rashly scrapping this successful and environmentally-sound transport technology. Many have since agreed that Melbourne's persistence was right.

As an engineer I have been glad to witness the rebirth of the tram in Europe and North America, and I have been impressed by the quality of the new systems I have seen as well as the contribution they are making to the problems of mobility in modern cities. It is pleasing to find such an effective blend of an established and tried technology with the latest innovations in propulsion systems, suspension, and trackwork, a fine example of incremental development.

Nottingham and its partners are to be warmly congratulated on the determination and commitment which have delivered their new transport system, but this little book tells much more than the story of the successful Nottingham project; it provides a wealth of information about the historical evolution of modern light rail transit".

Alec Broers
June 2007

*Nottingham newspaper reports the 'end of the trams' in 1936.*

## Chapter 1 R.I.P. Trams?

In the early hours of a September morning in 1936, Nottingham's people said what they thought was a final goodbye to their electric trams. As was to happen in many other cities, the Chairman of the Passenger Transport Committee drove the last car through excited crowds before it was stripped by travellers wanting souvenirs. Special tickets were issued lettered 'R.I.P'.

The last tram 'came home in triumph', wrote the *Nottingham Evening Post* on Monday 7 September. The City had "…enjoyed faithful service for many years, and the final tram car … closed a notable chapter in the history of Nottingham's transport undertaking". The Lord Mayor, addressing the large crowd, said that he had seen the first horse tram in Nottingham, 'but did not anticipate that he would see the end of trams'. The celebrations were marred at the end when a Councillor and the General Manager, Mr James Gunn, stepping hurriedly aside, fell into a depot inspection pit, and were 'shaken and bruised'. This incident had tragic consequences: Mr Gunn never fully recovered from his injuries and died three years later at the age of only 42.

As they carried home their tickets and trophies that Sunday morning, none of the thousands present is likely to have thought that rail transport would ever return to the City's streets. But this is the story of another transport revolution which brought the tram back to Nottingham, on Great Britain's fifth new-generation electric tramway. With the catchy trading name 'NET' (for Nottingham Express Transit), light rail is now playing an important part in revitalising the City.

Lying in the East Midlands of England, less than two hours train ride from London, Nottingham has about 275,000 residents, but 'Greater' Nottingham, with well over half a million, is the sixth largest urban area in the United Kingdom outside London. Employment in the area has changed fundamentally, with the ending, for example, of much manufacturing, including the bicycle industry which was once one of the biggest trades. Coal mining, another staple industry, has also almost completely disappeared. On the other hand employment in the service sector, including financial services, tourism, and retailing, is now most significant, and retail floor space in the centre grew by nearly half in the 1990s:

Nottingham now occupies fifth place amongst shopping destinations in Great Britain, and the City has firmly established itself – like Leeds and Birmingham in their respective areas – as the dominant regional centre. Cultural and entertainment opportunities have hugely grown, and the many city-centre venues attract patrons from a wide area. Further and higher education have also developed since the 1950s, with the establishment of the City's second university and the substantial expansion of the original Nottingham University: the two institutions together teach over 50,000 students on several campuses, with major flows of students to and fro each day.

One effect of such changes has been to increase city centre employment which now exceeds 55,000, and therefore to enlarge the travel-to-work area. Strong retail activity attracts customers from a large area of eastern England. To cater for the increasing volume of travel, improved public transport was seen as essential, and was strongly supported by both City and County Councils: a good start was made with park-and-ride schemes linked to dedicated bus services. The older Forest and Phoenix Park park-and-ride sites are now served by NET, and three more have been built as part of the first phase of the light rail project.

NET is part of the reinvention of central Nottingham, associated with pedestrianisation to provide a more pleasant environment for shoppers and strollers, and with the overhaul of all aspects of the streetscape. High-quality paving, new street furniture, and related landscaping have contributed to this improvement. The perception of modern tramways as sleek, stylish, and an asset to the urban scene is well understood in Europe and North America, and NET imitated European models as a symbol of Nottingham's ambitions. The visibility and permanence of light rail is another important consideration encouraging long-term business investment.

It would be wrong to overlook Nottingham's problems in an optimistic recital of its achievements, and it has been argued that there are in effect two cities here, the other of which suffers from many of the difficulties associated with twenty-first century urban life. NET seeks to reinforce the City's business success, but also has a role in turning round relative failure of other parts of Nottingham's past record. By improving access to work, for example from the Hyson Green district – designated a Government Task Force Area – the tramway is expected to play a part in wider urban regeneration and in reducing social exclusion.

# Chapter 2 A Famous Transport Heritage

Nottingham is one of few cities in Great Britain with an unbroken institutional record of local public transport operation. Nottingham City Transport, a partner in the operation of the present NET light rail system, has existed continuously since October 1897, when Nottingham Corporation acquired the undertaking of the Nottingham and District Tramways Company.

## The horse tram era 1878 – 1902

Local tramways in Nottingham were first considered in 1875. After negotiations and legal processes – far quicker, clearly, than present-day procedures – statutory powers for the construction and operation of horse tramways were granted in 1877, and Nottingham's first tramway era began when two services opened in September 1878. They ran from St Peter's Church near the Market Place, southwards via Carrington Street and Arkwright Street to Trent Bridge, with a branch along Station Street to London Road. The latter route served Nottingham's two principal railway stations, the Midland Railway station then facing Station Street, and the Great Northern Railway's newer London Road station. NET's present terminus at Station Street is situated almost above the route of one of Nottingham's first tramways.

A second part of the horse tram system opened in August 1879, and ran northwards from the Market Place along Milton Street and Mansfield Road to St John's Church, Carrington. Oddly enough, although the town centre terminals of the two lines were close together, the sections were not physically connected. The northern system was further extended in June 1881 with the opening of a second line from the Market Place, via Derby Road, Alfreton Road and Radford Road to Basford. The inward line of the new tramway follows the route of this 1881 line along part of Radford Road, and much of the present route of NET shadows the nineteenth-century line and its electric successor. The final extension to the horse tram system was a line opened in September 1881 along Forest Road linking the Carrington and Basford routes. The horse tram system was now complete, amounting to about 7.5 route miles, of which rather more than half was double line. Additional trams were bought as traffic grew: a total of 43 trams was eventually acquired, the last in 1895, of which 38 were in use at any one time.

*Left: This atmospheric view shows tired-looking Nottingham horse tram No 11 on the Trent Bridge service in Arkwright Street crossing the Midland Railway, not far from the present NET route. The car was built by Stephenson of New York in 1879, and its design is typical of the early phase in horse tram design, with a central longitudinal 'knife-board' seat on the upper deck.*
*Courtesy of Nottingham Historical Film Unit and www.picturethepast.org.uk*

*Right: Track-laying through most of Nottingham's main streets was a huge task, completed remarkably quickly in 1900-2.*
*This is Long Row adjoining the Market Place in 1902, and today's tramway runs up Market Street, straight ahead, then a single line only. Scenes not unlike this were to be repeated a century later.*
*Courtesy of J W Briggs and www.picturethepast.org.uk (NGTM008406)*

# Electric trams 1901 - 1936

Under the general provisions of the Tramways Act 1870, British local authorities could compulsorily acquire tramways within their jurisdiction after the expiration of twenty-one years from their date of authorisation, and Nottingham Corporation bought the horse tram undertaking in October 1897 for the sum of £80,000. They shortly afterwards sent deputations to study nine of the existing mechanically-powered undertakings, including the cable system at Edinburgh and the new electric systems at Bristol and Dover, and in 1899 powers were granted to electrify and extend Nottingham's tramways. The first electric trams, using the overhead system, entered public service in January 1901 on a new line through Carrington to Sherwood, and electric trams replaced horse on an extended route to Basford and Bulwell in July 1901. The northern and southern sections were soon connected by new track, and electric trams ran through the centre to Trent Bridge and Station Street from October 1901.

The last horse tram ran in April 1902 along Forest Road, the final horse route built and the only one not replaced by electric trams. Over the next quarter century electric tramways were built along most of the other main roads radiating from the centre, serving Colwick Road, Carlton, St Ann's Well, Mapperley, Arnold, Bulwell, Lenton, and Wilford Bridge. The last new sections were opened to Westdale Lane, Mapperley in 1926 and to Wollaton Park Gates in 1927. There were eventually twelve different lines, totalling 25.9 route miles (42 km). Unusually in Great Britain Nottingham also saw trams of an inter-urban route operated by the Nottinghamshire and Derbyshire Tramway Company, a 15 mile (24 km) route between Nottingham and Ripley which was reputedly the longest in England outside London. Trolleybuses replaced these company trams in 1933, and lasted until 1953. Nottingham's last twenty traditional trams were delivered by English Electric in 1926-7, and were only about ten years old when number 190 closed the last route from Arnold early on Sunday 6 September 1936. Most of these newest cars were sold to Aberdeen Corporation, and some continued in use until 1950.

*Tracks returned to Market Street in 2004: a northbound tram follows the same path as the 1900 rails, passing some of the original buildings.*

*Electric trams skirt the Market Square in 1910: today's tramway enters the picture from Beastmarket Hill at the lower right and passes up Market Street to the pillared Theatre Royal in the distance. Tram No 76 (in the foreground) was one of Nottingham's first series of bogie cars delivered in 1902, and was the only one of the class to be fitted later with an all-enclosed upper deck, an unusual feature at the time. Courtesy of Nottingham City Council and www.picturethepast.org.uk (NTGM008969)*

*Trams to and from Trent Bridge pass each other in this busy scene in Arkwright Street in 1928, with fully-enclosed car No 196 on the right nearing the end of its long journey on service 3 from Bulwell Market, now served by Nottingham's new tramway. The tram was barely two years old when photographed, having been delivered by English Electric in 1926. Sold to Aberdeen in 1936 the car enjoyed a long second life in Scotland. This street was served by horse trams from 1878, and electric trams from 1910 to 1934. Courtesy of Nottingham Historical Film Unit and www.picturethepast.org.uk (NTGM000199)*

## Horses and electricity

Although it may seem a primitive technology to us, the horse tramway was one of the decisive inventions of the nineteenth century, helping to make possible the wider separation of homes and work and encouraging the enlargement and improvement of many of our towns and cities. The critical characteristic of the horse tram was one it shares with modern light rail transit: the much reduced rolling resistance of metal wheels on metal rails meant that far less energy was required to move a load, so that two horses could haul a tram with about 45 seats, but a bus with only 25. The earliest British horse tramway systems were in Liverpool and London, beginning in 1869 and 1870 respectively, so Nottingham was not far behind, but with 316 horses and 37 trams in 1897, the undertaking was a modest one (the North Metropolitan Street Tramways Company, only one of a number of such undertakings in London, had 673 trams and 7167 horses at about the same period).

In 1889-90, just before electric traction became firmly established, the 811 route miles of tramway and 3801 trams in Great Britain were used by over 488 million passengers, so it will be clear that this was no minor transport operation. But horse traction was far from ideal. Each horse could only work for about four or five hours a day, so for each tram around ten horses were needed, working in relays. The cost of their feed, housing, and care was immense, and there were severe limits on the maximum possible size of vehicles. Once electric traction became technically feasible after about 1890 it offered huge advantages, including higher speed, better acceleration, the possibility of far larger cars, and the use of motive power remotely produced rather than being carried around with the vehicles themselves.

Between 1890 and 1914 electric tramways opened in almost every city and large town in Great Britain, with a peak in 1927 of some 14,500 trams on over 200 different undertakings. First horse and then electric tramways shaped many of the cities and towns we know today.

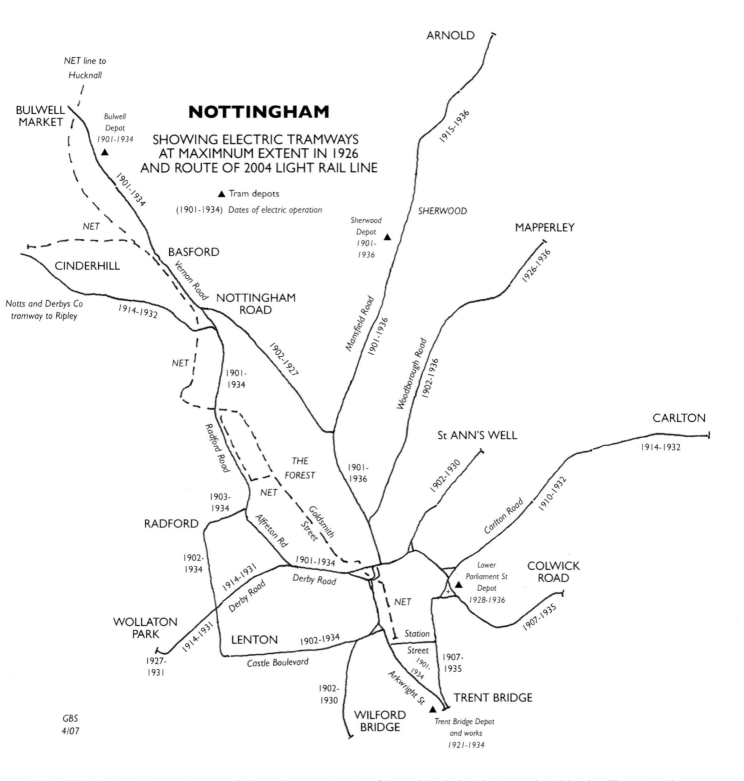

**NOTTINGHAM**

SHOWING ELECTRIC TRAMWAYS
AT MAXIMNUM EXTENT IN 1926
AND ROUTE OF 2004 LIGHT RAIL LINE

▲ Tram depots

(1901-1934) Dates of electric operation

*NET line to Hucknall*

ARNOLD

BULWELL MARKET

*Bulwell Depot 1901-1934*
▲

1901-1934

*NET*

CINDERHILL

BASFORD

*Vernon Road*

NOTTINGHAM ROAD

*Notts and Derbys Co tramway to Ripley*

1914-1932

1915-1936

SHERWOOD

*Sherwood Depot 1901-1936*
▲

MAPPERLEY

1926-1936

*NET*

1902-1927

1901-1934

*Mansfield Road*

1901-1936

*Woodborough Road*

1902-1936

*Radford Road*

THE FOREST

1901-1936

St ANN'S WELL

CARLTON

1914-1932

1903-1934

*NET*

*Goldsmith Street*

1902-1930

*Carlton Road*

1910-1932

RADFORD

*Alfreton Rd*

COLWICK ROAD

1902-1934

1914-1931

*Derby Road*

*Derby Road*

1901-1934

*Lower Parliament St Depot 1928-1936*
▲

*NET*

1907-1935

WOLLATON PARK

1914-1931

LENTON

1902-1934

*Castle Boulevard*

*Station Street 1901-1934*

1907-1935

1927-1931

*Arkwright St*

1902-1930

*GBS 4/07*

WILFORD BRIDGE

TRENT BRIDGE

*Trent Bridge Depot and works 1921-1934*
▲

*Little of Nottingham's new tramway follows the exact route of the original electric trams, but this plan illustrates the comparative routing of old and new.*

*Electric traction still served the north of Nottingham in the 1960s: two trolleybuses pass the old Public Hall in Highbury Road, Bulwell on a chilly December Sunday in 1962. They will turn back to Trent Bridge at Bulwell Market Place a short distance away, and their destination signs have already been changed.*
*The leading vehicle, No 552, was one of a large post-war batch of buses and was delivered in 1950. NET restored electric transport to this corridor, and the line passes beneath this road just beyond the second trolleybus, with the present Bulwell stop situated to the right. (Geoffrey Skelsey)*

## Trolleybuses 1927 – 1966

Nottingham was amongst the pioneers of extensive trolleybus operation in Great Britain. After studying the system in Birmingham which had replaced the Nechells tram line in 1922, the Corporation opened their first service in April 1927 with ten solid-tyred vehicles running between the Market Place and Nottingham Road, New Basford, replacing a partly single-track tramway. Following significant and profitable growth in traffic on this initial route, further tram routes were replaced by trolleybuses – initially called 'Railless' locally -- in 1930, and eleven different radial routes were converted in the following years, with some trolleybus services extending beyond the former limits of the trams. The final trolleybus conversion took place in 1935, and the last two tram services – to Mapperley and Arnold – were replaced by motorbuses in 1936, partly perhaps because both had sections lying outside the city boundary and the suburban local authority were opposed to trolley vehicles. More importantly, however, the appointment of the motor-bus advocate James Gunn as General Manager in 1934, and powerful political opposition, meant that as early as 1938 doubt was cast on the retention of trolleybuses in Nottingham and to an extent the system laboured for the rest of its life under a partial shadow of official scepticism. Despite numerous proposals which would, if implemented, have created a very large trolleybus network extending well beyond the City boundary, the system was in the event never significantly extended. Nottingham's trolleybus fleet eventually reached a maximum of 157 vehicles, making it the eighth largest fleet in the United Kingdom, and some fine new buses were delivered as late as 1952. A decision to abandon was taken in March 1961, and although most of the network survived until 1965, the last trolleybuses ran in June 1966.

## NCT buses: a factor in NET's success?

After experiments as early as 1906, and a pioneering operation by West Bridgford Urban District Council beginning in 1914, Nottingham's first permanent motorbus service was inaugurated to Bagthorpe in 1920, with three 40 h.p. single-deck buses.

Although, as we have seen, trolleybuses took over much of Nottingham's trunk tramway network, as early as 1938 there were substantially more motor buses than trolleybuses in the fleet. Motor buses were initially used principally on feeder services, but the use of diesel-engined buses to replace trams on the main Mapperley and Arnold services marked a change of policy, and no further trolleybus routes were inaugurated. After 1966 Nottingham was entirely a motor bus operation. The undertaking began to introduce one-person operation in 1970, a process almost complete by 1977, and in the previous year the fleet had reached an all-time maximum of 494 operational vehicles.

The latest phase in the 110 year history of Nottingham City Transport may have influenced the success of light rail in the city. The radical Thatcher government elected in 1979 overturned the status quo in the British bus industry in two ways. In the first place the existing state-owned bus operations in England and Wales were sold, and local authorities were encouraged (although never compelled) to divest themselves of ownership of their bus undertakings. Nottingham was one of the major local authority operators which retained ownership of its bus operations, although it was required to transfer them to an arms-length subsidiary, Nottingham City Transport Limited, which was registered in March 1986 and continues in existence in 2007.

In the second place, bus and coach services outside London were deregulated, and in 1986 the exclusive operating rights enjoyed by existing undertakings, generally since 1931 but for far longer in some towns and cities including Nottingham, were abolished. However, Nottingham in fact experienced relatively little on-the-road competition from other operators, and NCT proved to be innovative in adapting its route structure, with a major reorganisation implemented in 2001. The undertaking has also been active in vehicle renewal, creating one of the youngest city fleets in Great Britain, and took advantage of the deregulated structure to acquire other concerns and to extend its operations well beyond its former limits.

The City Council retained sole ownership of its enlarged network until 2001 when a modest share was issued to a French-registered transport operator, Transdev plc, a member (with NCT) of the Arrow Consortium which – as we shall see – created NET, and which has considerable experience in operating both bus and tram systems in Great Britain and overseas. In 2007 NCT had a fleet of about 375 buses, mainly with low-floor access. It is now the largest of the fourteen remaining local-authority owned bus undertakings in Great Britain. NCT's participation in the NET operation, and its predominance in bus operation locally, has facilitated the creation of an inter-linked light rail/bus system, and light rail's success in building traffic beyond expectations must derive in part from effective inter-modal integration.

*The operations of Nottingham City Transport Ltd link effectively with NET trams. No 545 on the right is running to Bulwell via the western part of the city, and will terminate close to the NET tram stop. It is a low-floor single deck Optare 'Excel' new in 2001, and appears in the undertaking's stylish and traditional green livery. 423 is a double-deck easy-access Dennis Trident, new in 2000. The buses stand in Milton Street outside the Victoria Centre and in the background is the handsome clock tower which is all that remains of the former Victoria station buildings.*

## So why did we get rid of the old trams and trolleybuses?

Nottingham's first electric trams disappeared after only thirty-five years, the trolleybuses after thirty-nine. New trams continued to be built elsewhere in Great Britain, and line extensions were opened in Glasgow, Leeds, and Sunderland as late as 1949, but the last English city tramway, in Sheffield, closed in 1960 and Glasgow's, the last in the United Kingdom, in 1962. Only the sea-side trams in Blackpool and the Isle of Man continued to operate.

Meanwhile in some overseas countries, notably Germany, the Netherlands, Switzerland, Austria, and Belgium, urban tramways continued to be developed with heavy investment in new vehicles and track.

Why did we discard transport modes which are now considered to have a future?

In Great Britain the principal reason was undoubtedly economic. Costs of labour and materials rose rapidly during and after the First World War, and tight local control on fares enabled politicians to refuse the increases needed to match the growing costs just as the initial equipment was wearing out. Substantial profits in earlier years had been devoted to local rate reductions rather than reinvested in the replacement of assets; the international trade recession after 1929 enforced rigid economy in local government expenditure. Meanwhile, at just this time, motor buses were improving rapidly, and with the introduction of diesel engines their size and operating cost more nearly approached those of trams. Also at this period trolleybuses, mostly with three axles, generally had ten or so more seats than motor buses, an important factor in explaining their attraction.

It became cheaper to replace trams with buses or trolleybuses than to renew the tramway equipment, even in those places (such as Birmingham, Liverpool, and Leeds) where significant lengths of segregated tracks meant that trams could still offer a superior service. Furthermore Britain's trams had, in most cases, relatively low capacity and therefore offered few advantages in terms of staff productivity. Although several British undertakings planned to retain and extend their tramways after the Second World War, by the 1950s declining passenger traffic and further cost increases led all the remaining city authorities to revise their policies. Despite their palpable environmental benefits, notably almost silent operation, trolleybuses too appeared to be more costly, and their old advantages diminished as larger motor buses became available. To a greater extent than any other major industrialised country, Great Britain became almost an 'all diesel bus' country after 1972 when the last trolleybus ran in Bradford.

# Chapter 3 The legacy of Nottingham's railways

The development of the first phase of NET – and its extension in future – are closely bound up with the layout and history of conventional railways in and around Nottingham, because the planning and construction of the light rail network has been strongly influenced by the availability of former railway rights-of-way.

## Making the most of the past

The re-use of these routes has become a critical factor in the creation of new light rail and tramway installations in many parts of the world. Routeways constructed a century or more ago into the heart of built-up areas are a priceless resource, and their availability has made possible cost-effective new transport links. All five of the new British tramways have, to a greater or lesser extent, made use of former railway alignments, as have one of the two 'LUAS' light rail lines in Dublin, and the somewhat heavier Docklands Light Railway and Tyne and Wear Metro.

Such reuse of railway routes is not new. For instance, most of the surviving Glenelg tramway in Adelaide, South Australia, was built over the former South Terrace railway line in 1929, and in Great Britain

This plan shows Nottingham's railways at their maximum extent, making clear how the built-up area was hardly served at all except by the 1899 Great Central line, mostly built in tunnel through the city centre. Nottingham's topography meant that routings were indirect, and the dates show how early most of the stations were closed: of all the many stations on this map, only one – Nottingham (Midland) – has remained continuously open, on three different sites. Railways played almost no part in local transport after 1914, but their expensively-built routeways offered the possibility of new transport uses. Regrettably most have been discarded.
The map clearly shows how the NET route cuts directly across the central area never served by railways.

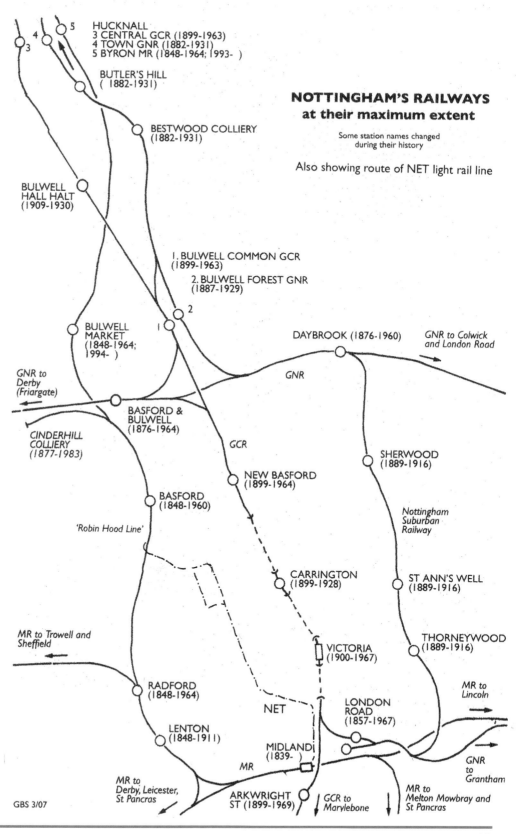

**NOTTINGHAM'S RAILWAYS at their maximum extent**

Some station names changed during their history

Also showing route of NET light rail line

HUCKNALL
3 CENTRAL GCR (1899-1963)
4 TOWN GNR (1882-1931)
5 BYRON MR (1848-1964; 1993- )

BUTLER'S HILL ( 1882-1931)

BESTWOOD COLLIERY (1882-1931)

BULWELL HALL HALT (1909-1930)

1. BULWELL COMMON GCR (1899-1963)
2. BULWELL FOREST GNR (1887-1929)

DAYBROOK (1876-1960)

GNR to Colwick and London Road

BULWELL MARKET (1848-1964; 1994- )

GNR to Derby (Friargate)

GNR

BASFORD & BULWELL (1876-1964)

CINDERHILL COLLIERY (1877-1983)

GCR

SHERWOOD (1889-1916)

NEW BASFORD (1899-1964)

Nottingham Suburban Railway

BASFORD (1848-1960)

'Robin Hood Line'

CARRINGTON (1899-1928)

ST ANN'S WELL (1889-1916)

MR to Trowell and Sheffield

VICTORIA (1900-1967)

THORNEYWOOD (1889-1916)

MR to Lincoln

RADFORD (1848-1964)

NET

LONDON ROAD (1857-1967)

LENTON (1848-1911)

MIDLAND (1839- )

MR

GBS 3/07

MR to Derby, Leicester, St Pancras

ARKWRIGHT ST (1899-1969)

GCR to Marylebone

MR to Melton Mowbray and St Pancras

GNR to Grantham

*This interior view of Victoria towards the end of its life gives an impression of its huge proportions: this area is now a low-roofed basement car park, interrupted by hundreds of concrete columns.*
*(Courtesy Robert Darlaston)*

*The reconstruction of the Robin Hood line marked a major step in the revival of Greater Nottingham's transport system. In 1998 a diesel train for Nottingham waits to leave Hucknall, a station reopened in 1993 after 29 years of closure.*

*Hucknall's new station was provided with generous car parking to encourage park-and-ride use.*

*By 2004 the NET line had taken over part of the car park and a large supermarket had been built in the background. NET and the Robin Hood trains complement each other over this section.*

the line of the Tyneside Tramways between Gosforth (Newcastle) and Wallsend, which opened in 1902, partly followed the route of the defunct Coxlodge Colliery waggonway.

Nottingham probably lost more of its railways and stations than any of Great Britain's major cities, with the possible exception of Sheffield, and the residue of abandoned rights of way may have seemed to offer a framework for a replacement transport system.

However, Nottingham's railway network, like that of most of Great Britain's cities, came into existence mainly to serve the needs of national passenger and freight transport, not local traffic. The City's geography, rising steeply from the valleys of the Trent and Leen, inhibited the creation of an urban rail system, and the earliest line – the Midland Counties Railway from Derby opened in 1839 – terminated in the valley below, not far from the present passenger station which is still some distance from the main business district. Later railways also skirted central Nottingham.

Only one railway had the potential to cater for local passenger traffic, the Nottingham Suburban Railway opened in 1889 around the eastern edge of the town, serving stations at Sherwood, St Ann's Well, and Thorneywood. But the layout of the line, with its circuitous route into the inconvenient London Road terminus, meant that the later establishment of direct electric tramways soon removed such passenger traffic as there had ever been. All three districts were served by tram by 1910, and the stations closed to passengers as a wartime measure in 1916, never to reopen. Although part at least of the route might have been usable for other public transport purposes, or as a cycle-way or green way, the cuttings were eventually partly infilled making the through route unusable.

A second lost line was the London extension of the Great Central Railway, which opened through Nottingham to London (Marylebone) in 1899. Building this required massive disruption, the last major main-line railway construction through a British city until the opening of the Channel Tunnel rail-link to St Pancras in 2007. Included was the vast new sub-surface Victoria station, opened in 1900.

Less than a lifetime later almost the whole Great Central route was abandoned in 1967-9, and the urban section in Nottingham was sold to the City, who reportedly also paid for a new junction at Loughborough to allow diversion of the remaining freight trains in July 1967. The Victoria Shopping Centre was built on the site of the station, its low basement car-park effectively severing the north-south route, and in addition the extensive railway lands in the Meadows district south of the centre were developed for housing.

## Why did railways close?

The wisdom of abandoning a significant proportion of Great Britain's passenger railways over the last fifty years is often questioned. But for most of their life Britain's railways operated in a harsh economic environment, and for a century or more were – in an urban context at least – subject to strong and effective competition. Decisions to withdraw passenger services, and sometimes wholly to abandon lines, were not taken lightly but took place in circumstances very different from today's: before 1968 either company shareholders or Parliament sought direct profitability from railway operation and demanded drastic cost reduction in order to achieve this. Revenue support, justified by the social benefits of local railways, is a relatively recent phenomenon, and was in fact one of the lesser-known proposals made in the much-maligned 'Beeching' Report of 1963. The narrow financial approach of the early 1960s lacked any long-term strategic vision, and the price for this is being paid today.

In Nottingham the early closure of Lenton station (in 1911) and the failure of the Suburban Line through Sherwood to establish itself, leading to its closure in 1916, are pointers to the ousting of local passenger trains by effective road transport. Of about twenty passenger stations once existing within and immediately around the City about half had already closed to passengers by 1960, before the much-criticised 'reshaping' plans, and several lines had been wholly abandoned, leaving a legacy of disused routes. The lines eventually partially incorporated into NET suffered different fates. The former Great Central Railway route, opened in 1899 and mainly closed by 1969, was not protected after the track was lifted and most became unavailable. On the other hand the Nottingham-Hucknall line, closed to passengers in 1964, remained in use for coal traffic and could be reused with less difficulty.

Three peripheral passenger stations survived in 1990 in Nottingham and its immediate environs, but only one (Beeston) handled substantial daily passenger traffic.

*A present-day Robin Hood train stands at Bulwell station, reopened in 1994, as a NET tram leaves in the background. In 2007 it was announced that a new operator would take over operation of this and other local train services. The Robin Hood Line branding is prominent on the platform surface.*

## Robin Hood to the rescue

The survival of the Nottingham – Hucknall railway and hence its availability to form the core of NET's Line One, was partly a matter of chance. When the passenger service closed in 1964 local stations at Radford, Basford, and Bulwell, had frequent bus or trolleybus services passing their doors, and in comparison nine daily trains in each direction, routed to the inconvenient Midland Station, appealed little to the daily passenger. However the double-track, signalled line remained in use for coal traffic from Linby, Newstead, and Calverton collieries to the huge generating stations in the Trent Valley. The collapse of the British deep-mined coal industry after 1985 threatened the survival of this railway as a freight route but also stimulated its revival for passenger trains, as the closure of most local collieries left grave social and employment problems which improved public transport would alleviate.

The project to reopen the line to passengers was launched in 1987. The first phase, from Nottingham through Hucknall to Newstead, was still in use for coal trains and cost some £1.73 million to rehabilitate, including rebuilt stations. Funding came mainly from Nottinghamshire County Council and the European Union's Regional Development Fund, and the local councils were originally involved closely in the promotion of the service. This section, branded the 'Robin Hood Line', opened in 1993, initially with hourly trains. The subsequent stages were implemented during and after the much-criticised privatisation of British Railways, and the eventual cost – amounting to some £20 million – was significantly increased by the new structure of the industry. The line through to Mansfield was opened in 1994, and the final section to Worksop in 1998. The 'Robin Hood' service is now used by some 3,250 passengers each day, or over a million a year, a not unimpressive result bearing in mind that there had been no rail service over the route for thirty years.

The revival of rail transport in the area was a triumph for pro-public transport policies of Nottinghamshire County Council, in association with Derbyshire County Council, Nottingham City Council, and British Rail and its successors. The whole line has been imaginatively marketed, and special emphasis was placed on large, monitored car-parks at stations, and on reliable feeder bus services, policies which were later extended to NET.

Robin Hood and NET are complementary projects, the first serving a regional role extending high quality public transport well beyond Nottingham and its environs, the latter in this context fulfilling a distributive role, enhancing the value of Robin Hood by providing (through interchange at Nottingham, Hucknall and Bulwell) convenient access to a wider range of objectives in the central area.

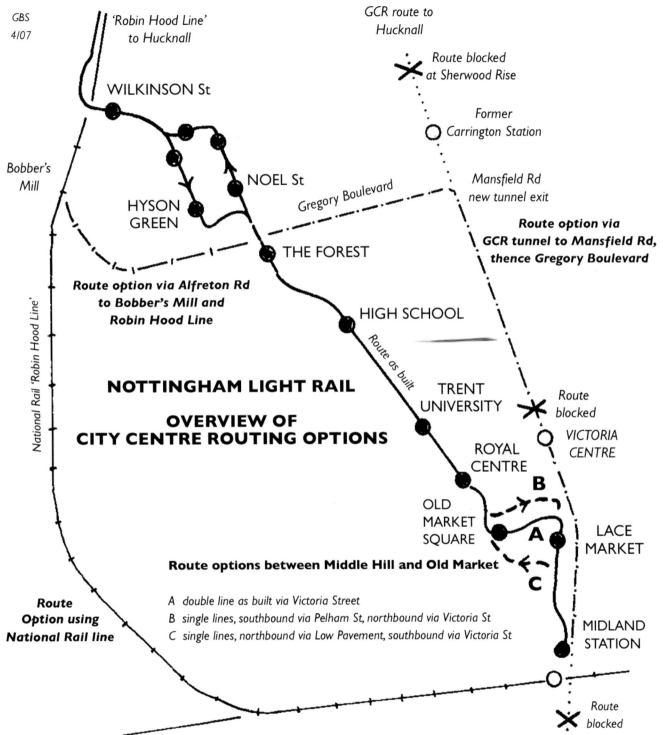

GBS
4/07

'Robin Hood Line'
to Hucknall

GCR route to
Hucknall

Route blocked
at Sherwood Rise

WILKINSON St

Former
Carrington Station

Bobber's
Mill

NOEL St

Gregory Boulevard

Mansfield Rd
new tunnel exit

HYSON
GREEN

Route option via
GCR tunnel to Mansfield Rd,
thence Gregory Boulevard

THE FOREST

Route option via Alfreton Rd
to Bobber's Mill and
Robin Hood Line

HIGH SCHOOL

Route as built

National Rail 'Robin Hood Line'

NOTTINGHAM LIGHT RAIL

OVERVIEW OF
CITY CENTRE ROUTING OPTIONS

TRENT
UNIVERSITY

Route
blocked

VICTORIA
CENTRE

ROYAL
CENTRE

B

OLD
MARKET
SQUARE

A

LACE
MARKET

Route
Option using
National Rail line

Route options between Middle Hill and Old Market

C

A  double line as built via Victoria Street
B  single lines, southbound via Pelham St, northbound via Victoria St
C  single lines, northbound via Low Pavement, southbound via Victoria St

MIDLAND
STATION

Route
blocked

This plan illustrates some of the options examined in planning NET: it shows the possible re-use of the former Great Central tunnels, with a new surface link from Mansfield Road towards Hyson Green and the Robin Hood Line, but the city centre coverage of this route would have been limited and the station and other works expensive. NET's on-street routing connected directly with many more traffic objectives.

# Chapter 4 The origins of NET

## Transport policies in 'the rail dark ages'

Development of urban transport in Great Britain did not wholly end in the period after the abandonment of tramways, trolleybuses, and many local railways in the 1960s. Occasional advocacy of well-established technologies, including what we now call light rail, continued. For example, studies for a light rail system in Birmingham took place as early as 1954, and the first formulation of what became the Midland Metro was published in 1966. In the same year similar studies took place in Sheffield, for the Yorkshire and Humberside Economic Planning Council. The idea of modern tramways never quite died, even if the term 'tram' was carefully eschewed in the early years and, as described in the Topic Box, where new fixed-track urban transport systems emerged in many parts of the world in the 1990s up-dated versions of the conventional tramway were – unexpectedly perhaps – often the preferred option.

What was lacking in Great Britain before 1968 was any plausible funding regime to contribute to the capital cost of such projects, and to provide revenue support. A national and local political and economic structure which contemplated closure of such existing rail routes as the electrified Liverpool – Southport

*Very little of the ex-GCR route was in fact reused, and only a short length of the original viaduct was rehabilitated. North of Canal Street a new concrete viaduct was constructed. In the distance the portal of Thurland Street tunnel formerly leading to Victoria can just be seen, although building work in 2007 will hide this view.*

*After joining the railway trackbed at Wilkinson Street NET required construction of two additional tracks as far as Bulwell. This view north of Basford shows how substantial some of the work was, requiring diversion of the River Leen on the left.*

and North London lines was unlikely enthusiastically to contemplate the creation of similar new enterprises. Indeed the 1966 Birmingham proposal was loftily dismissed by the responsible City Councillor as 'needing a subsidy…' and hence '..inefficient..'. A turnaround in official attitudes occurred over a similar period in a number of countries including some, such as France and Canada, where the conventional tramway had disappeared almost as completely as from Great Britain. The principle of British central government capital grants towards public transport (as distinct from road) projects was at last realised in the Transport Act 1968, opening the way to a period of fervent planning, and even to some realised projects. However, eligibility for such grants was restricted and a Nottingham infrastructure project – even if one had matured – is unlikely to have qualified.

At this period, transport planning in Nottingham was based on a Highway Plan drawn up in 1966, *Traffic in Nottingham 1965-2000*, which envisaged a network of urban motorways involving widespread property demolition. In this respect the City resembled most others in the developed world. This was the era of a widespread belief that the vitality and business success of cities depended on unrestricted car access, but this was changing. It began to be realised that if society would not, or could not, remodel cities to accommodate unrestricted motor traffic, then a system of priorities had to be established instead. In short, full motorisation was in practice impossible without destroying the very cities it was intended to serve. In Great Britain the Buchanan Report (1963), despite persistent misrepresentation ever since, first argued this point, as well as floating the idea of road pricing.

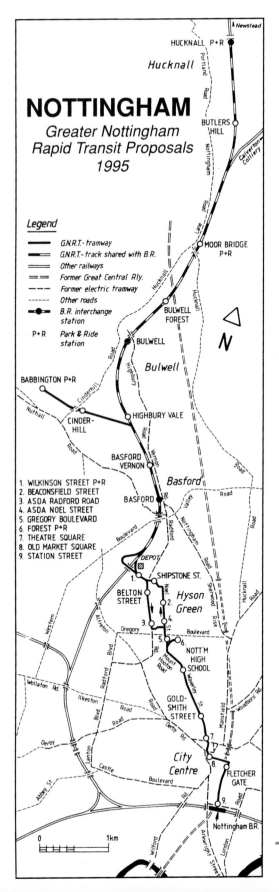

## NOTTINGHAM
### Greater Nottingham Rapid Transit Proposals 1995

**Legend**

| | |
|---|---|
| ▬▬▬ | G.N.R.T.- tramway |
| ▬▬▬ | G.N.R.T.- track shared with B.R. |
| ═══ | Other railways |
| ══ | Former Great Central Rly. |
| ----- | Former electric tramway |
| ------- | Other roads |
| ●━●━● | B.R. interchange station |
| P+R | Park & Ride station |

1. WILKINSON STREET P+R
2. BEACONSFIELD STREET
3. ASDA RADFORD ROAD
4. ASDA NOEL STREET
5. GREGORY BOULEVARD
6. FOREST P+R
7. THEATRE SQUARE
8. OLD MARKET SQUARE
9. STATION STREET

0      1km

After the controversial and destructive building of the first section of Nottingham's inner city highway, seductively called 'Maid Marion Way', popular resistance to reshaping the City was growing in strength and when a Public Inquiry into plans for a second section of new road (which would predictably have been named 'Robin Hood Way') was held in May 1970 the opponents prevailed. Political changes in Nottingham in 1972 led to a change of attitude, and in October 1972 a new transport policy was announced. This emphasised pedestrianisation, restraint on car use, and the improvement of public transport.

A free circular city centre bus service was inaugurated later that year, and within months was working at sixty per cent capacity. Most important, though, was an entirely novel 'traffic collar' system, devised to limit private motoring into the city centre in order to ensure operational priority for buses, thus making them more attractive. Bus frequencies were also improved, and a system of vehicle actuation of traffic signals introduced to facilitate reliable operation of the city centre free buses. This project was thought likely to be more effective than the contemporary introduction of dedicated bus lanes, notably in Reading, which were already rebalancing the road system slightly in favour of public transport.

Deploying what was for the period a sophisticated system of centralised monitoring of traffic lights, the Nottingham collar scheme used controlled signal phases to regulate vehicle access in proportion to the overall volume of traffic, and in particular, to facilitate the free movement of buses. The delay imposed on queuing motorists was expected to encourage diversion to peripheral car parks and the free bus.

This project, which attracted considerable attention from contemporary planners, involved many practical difficulties, and although modestly successful in achieving its traffic-flow objectives, drew such passionate opposition from motorists and traders that it was eventually abandoned. Technically, it was perhaps ahead of its time, but the scheme nonetheless showed that there was an alternative approach to managing traffic in towns. In 1974 there appeared in its wake what may be the earliest formulation of the project which eventually materialised as NET.

*This map illustrates the basis of the parliamentary powers to build Line One, although when published the possibility of some track-sharing north of Wilkinson Street was still envisaged. This was later found not to be cost-effective. Some stop names were later changed, but this is broadly the line as built in 2000-3. (Courtesy Tramways and Urban Transit)*

## The turning of the tide: the tram makes a comeback

As we have seen, in the 1960s the conventional tramway was widely believed to be an obsolescent technology. With notable exceptions, it appeared to be in final decline in most of the world: in each of Great Britain and Canada only one undertaking remained, in the United States seven, in France three. Regular trams disappeared completely from Spain, Denmark, and New Zealand. The turning point came quite suddenly and unexpectedly, stimulated by the oil crisis of 1973 (which changed political attitudes and relative costs), by ambitions for city centre renewal, and by a realisation that updated light rail systems offered major advantages in terms of speedy achievability, cost effectiveness, and environmental quality. Two new undertakings with light rail features opened, in Edmonton in Canada in 1978, and in Newcastle-upon-Tyne in England in 1980, both using light rail vehicles and both partly using former railway routes. They were followed by further entirely new systems in Calgary in Canada and San Diego in California in 1981, and in Nantes in France in 1985, each of which – in a decisive break with the past – re-introduced partly street-based operation.

Since 1981 the status of tramways or light rail transit has been transformed. By 2006 there were seven new light rail installations operating in Great Britain, eleven in France, and fifteen in the United States, with more being planned or under construction. Symbolically, and significantly, trams have returned to four European capital cities, Paris, London, Dublin, and Athens, from which they had previously vanished up to seventy years ago. Of the 27 capitals of the enlarged European Union, all but six now have at least some tramways. Between 1988 and 1994 the UK Parliament approved construction of new tram or light rail systems in seven British cities, the last one in Nottingham. This reversal of fortune would have seemed inconceivable when the City's original trams last ran fifty eight years before.

## The first stirrings

Writing in the journal *Modern Tramway* in May 1974, the late J H Price, perhaps the most thoughtful writer on light rail and tramway topics of the period, proposed the reuse of the former Great Central Railway tunnels beneath central Nottingham for a local transit system. Bearing in mind the obstructive basement of the Victoria Centre, this would have required a costly by-pass tunnel alongside the new development, and initially separate lines were proposed northwards to Bulwell, Basford and Cinderhill, southwards towards Ruddington, and eastwards on the former GN route towards Colwick. These would link a spread of peripheral car parks directly to the major new shopping centres at Victoria and the Broad Marsh. This was an astonishingly prescient forecast of much that actually happened a quarter century later, although without the use of the tunnels. Regrettably the proposal went no further, and subsequently the railway route southwards was built over, and the northern part of the urban tunnels was filled in.

Public transport surveys in the 1960s revealed that Nottingham's heaviest bus traffic was on routes serving the densest residential areas to the north and north-west, as well as to the south over the Trent bridges. Unsurprisingly these are precisely the routings selected four decades later for NET and its extensions, and were clearly those where drastic action seemed to be called for if Nottingham was not to seize up. In 1987 the setting up of Nottingham Development Enterprise started a process of addressing such issues, and re-examining the means by which other cities in Europe and North America had set about regenerating themselves. As described in the Topic Box above, by this time light rail operation had already begun around Newcastle upon Tyne, and street-based trams had returned to Calgary, San Diego, and Nantes. The new body, supported by both City and County Councils and by the Nottingham Chamber of Commerce, identified modern public transport systems as one important factor bringing about change in cities, and in the autumn of 1988 a feasibility study began which reviewed available transport modes and named the corridors likely to benefit from a new system. In February 1989 consultants advised that light rail transit was the preferred mode and that the north-western corridor towards Hucknall and Cinderhill was the best prospect. NET had been conceived.

## Track or route sharing?

In planning NET a fundamental choice lay between shared use of existing railway lines and wholly independent operation, albeit making use of railway routeways. Line One as built exemplifies a critical advantage of modern light rail systems. Use of a railway routeway at the outer end of the line provides relatively fast transit free from road congestion. Transferring to on-street operation towards the centre provides slower travel subject to signalled intersections, but greatly improves accessibility and penetration through frequent stops situated a few paces from major traffic objectives. It was this happy match of characteristics that led to a major change in light rail planning, beginning in Germany but now spreading to other countries, the concept of the 'tram-train'. Starting in Nottingham's twin city of Karlsruhe in 1991, such projects introduce light rail services over local 'heavy' rail lines, linking these to town-centre tramways  thus providing direct service into the centres and eliminating a change of mode at possibly peripheral city stations (like Nottingham's). One such scheme was later introduced in Great Britain in 2002, when the Tyne and Wear Metro was extended over the National Rail line to Sunderland, interworking with conventional diesel trains.

This principle was thoroughly considered in the 1990s for what became the NET route between Bulwell and Hucknall. To seek clarification of the issues that would arise were the two modes to share tracks, at that time an unknown concept in Great Britain, the then consultancy arm of British Rail were contracted to investigate the operation of trams and trains together along part of the Robin Hood Line. This would have had the advantage of preserving double-track operation the whole length of the new route, and of facilitating simpler interchange between trams and trains.

However such interworking involves significant problems. Tramcars normally have much lower end-loading and impact resistance properties than conventional trains, and there are also issues involving different buffer height above rail level. Whilst (as in Tyne and Wear) modern train protection signalling systems can practically eliminate the risk of end-on collisions, although at significant additional expense, other considerations involve different floor heights, body widths, and the differing standards of wheel profiles for trains and street-running trams, important especially at pointwork. Finally, the practical scheduling and operational issues involved in running distinct and separately-managed services over the same tracks cannot be ignored, especially in the modern British context.

The studies in the early 1990's clarified the technical issues involved, and showed that constructional costs would be lessened were shared track to be used, especially if expensive land-take was thereby reduced. However operational costs were expected to be greater, and the balance of advantage in the

*The Tyne and wear Metro opened in 1980 is wholly segregated but it uses light rail techniques and vehicles based on German 'Stadtbahn' principles. It paved the way for further developments in Great Britain.*

Nottingham context was eventually found to lie with separate tracks rather than shared use. As built NET shares the Robin Hood line route, but not its tracks.

## Route evaluation

The determination of the line of phase one of the new tramway involved permutations of the two rail alignments – as we have seen, the remains of the former GCR viaduct and tunnels, and the Robin Hood Line – with selection of an optimal street running section between them. In the period after 1989 a number of options emerged, of which the principal choice was between a part-tunnel option and an all-street option. The choices were:

■ A route using the ex GCR viaduct and tunnels from Midland Station to a point near the north end of the Mansfield Road tunnel beyond the Victoria Station site, including the costly diversion around the Victoria Centre and a new tunnelled exit from the tunnel on to surface reservation alongside Gregory Avenue in the Forest Recreation Ground. In order to minimise conflict with road traffic, the line would then – largely as eventually built – follow separate inward and outward routes in Noel Street and Radford Road, rejoining at Wilkinson Street and then using the Robin Hood Line northwards.

■ Different surface routes between Middle Hill (just north of the Midland Station) and the Old Market, involving single one-direction tracks in Low Pavement and Wheeler Gate, or Victoria Street, or Pelham Street. Common to these lines was a core section through the Old Market Place past the Theatre Royal to The Forest.

■ North of the Forest further options were considered, with tracks via Noel Street and Radford Road (as built), or via Gregory Boulevard and Alfreton Road, joining the Robin Hood Line at Bobber's Mill, further south than Wilkinson Street.

These options are summarised on the map, and it will be clear that the street-based option serves a far wider range of traffic objectives, although it required vehicles able to adapt to relatively steep gradients and sharp curves.

Use of the former Great Central route north of Nottingham, which also leads directly to Hucknall, was effectively ruled out for ever by the disposal of successive parcels of the track for house building, notably at Sherwood Rise, New Basford, and Bagthorpe where substantial residential developments now occupy the former railway. Examination of the disused GCR tunnels themselves found them to be in relatively good condition despite over thirty years of neglect, although Thurland Street tunnel just south of Victoria,

*The first Calgary light rail line opened in 1981, also using German-pattern light rail vehicles. By adopting street running in the city centre the system broke decisively with conventional attitudes to tramways and was in a sense one progenitor of NET.*

on a stretch which might have been re-used, showed some deterioration through water penetration. The critical point, as we have seen, would have been the need to build a substantial diversionary tunnel beneath or around the Victoria Centre, where use of the original route was prevented by the closely spaced columns supporting the shops and flats above. Apart from the high cost of construction, estimated at first to be £12 million, new regulations for underground railway stations introduced in the aftermath of the King's Cross underground station fire in 1987, hugely increased the complexity of such installations, and hence their construction and operating cost. These factors would probably have prevented there being more than one city centre stop, so access from the new line would not have been particularly convenient. There were also planning arguments in favour of displacing the line westwards through the Old Market area in order to strengthen the retail area west of the Victoria Centre, and to serve Nottingham Trent University.

All in all these considerations cast doubt on the substantial use of the former GCR route through the City, not least because of its cost and the limited access it would offer to the city centre. Shared use of at least part of the Robin Hood Line remained a possibility into the early 1990s, with four tracks being proposed where the formation could be widened, but at this stage with NET using the outermost tracks and serving additional stops, and conventional trains the innermost pair. Fully shared use of double track was intended north of Highbury Vale. In the event, for the reasons we have already seen, this option was eventually abandoned in favour of separate pairs of tracks as far as Bulwell, and separate single lines thereafter. Given the operational and financial issues involving the National Rail network since the late 1990s this may well have been a fortuitous decision, although single line working of both trams and trains involves some constraints.

## Promotion and realisation

The establishment in 1991 of a joint venture company, Greater Nottingham Rapid Transit Ltd, with representation of the County and City Councils and Nottingham Development Enterprise, provided the formal framework and the capitalisation to carry the project forward through its development stage (NET has benefited from consistent and broad political support, in contrast to some other projects). After being deposited in Parliament as a Bill in November 1991, the Greater Nottingham Light Rapid Transit Act received Royal Assent on 21 July 1994, the same day as the Croydon Tramlink Act. These were historic enactments since they were the last entirely new tramways in Great Britain to be authorised under the nineteenth century Tramways Act procedure, thereafter superseded by Orders made under the Transport and Works Act 1992.

*Street trams first returned to a British city in 1992 with the opening of the new Manchester system. Four more new systems followed.*

The promoters invited tenders for the procurement of the new tram system, and selected Arrow Light Rail Ltd as a special-purpose company to fund, design, build, operate and maintain the first line. Arrow's funding is secured by a Private Finance Initiative, for which HM Government approved credit authority in December 1998. Once this funding was in place the way was open for detailed negotiations on construction and procurement, and following signature of contracts in May 2000 construction work began the following month with the laying of a commemorative stone in the Old Market Square by the then Transport Minister.

The promoters awarded the design-built-operate concession for a period of 30.5 years. The funding package is believed to have been the largest public transport PFI arrangement made at that time. The Consortium is made up of six partners, each with particular expertise relevant to the project. The partners are:

- Bombardier (originally ADtranz) once a railway rolling-stock builder but now with wider expertise in all aspects of rail systems. (12.5 per cent)

- Carillion Private Finance, part a group with extensive interests in transport and civil construction, deriving originally from the well-known Tarmac company. (12.5 per cent)

- Transdev, a transport management company based in France, and with experience of some seventy public transport undertakings, including modern tramways. (12.5 per cent)

- Nottingham City Transport Ltd. (12.5 per cent)

- Innisfree, an infrastructure investment group, with particular experience in PFI projects. (30 per cent)

- Galaxy Fund, a public transport infrastructure investor. (20 per cent)

Arrow let a 42 month fixed price turnkey construction contract to a consortium comprising ADtranz (later Bombardier) and Carillion Construction for the design and building of the tramway and associated works. ADtranz provided the trams, power, signalling and communications systems, and Carillion the civil engineering, track and tram stops. Work started in 2001 with utility diversion and alterations to the 'railway' section where major civil engineering work was required to create a widened formation. Part of the former railway viaduct between Weekday Cross and Station Street also had to be rebuilt. Track laying started at Hyson Green in October 2001 and by the end of 2002 track had been completed on the 'railway' sections. The depot was occupied from September 2002. Wiring on the railway sections began immediately, and was energized as far as Highbury Vale in March 2003. By late 2003 track and wiring were complete throughout. Trial running began on the railway section in March 2003, with tram No 202 making the first powered run from Wilkinson Street as far as Highbury Vale. No 208 followed with a powered test run to Station Street on 31 August, a few days short of sixty-seven years since the 'final tram car' of 1936. A 'ceremonial' first tram ran on 10 September. Final opening was delayed by minor derailments during test running in May and September 2003, which called for remedial work, including modification of the points operating mechanisms. Following this a shadow timetable began operation early in 2004 to familiarize both tram drivers and the general public and motorists with the reality of tram operation.

The operation of the completed system was conceded to the Nottingham Tram Consortium, consisting of Nottingham City Transport Ltd and Transdev Ltd, who will maintain and operate the system for 27 years. The official opening was performed by Alastair Darling MP, Secretary of State for Transport, on 8 March 2004, with the Lord Mayor and many other local dignitaries in attendance and a good deal of celebratory jollification, including bands and colourful banners in the city centre. Number 203, the first public service tram, left Phoenix Park at 05.58 on Tuesday 9 March 2004, with a large contingent of enthusiasts, staff, and media representatives. Number 214 followed with the 06.02 from Hucknall. NET was alive at last.

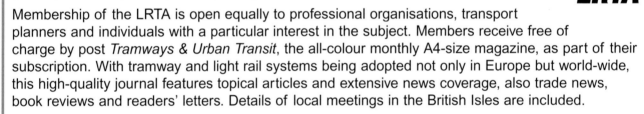

# Photo Interlude: Building NET

Local photographer Martin Cobley studied NET closely throughout the three-year period of construction and testing, and his pictures reveal the gradual emergence of Nottingham's new tramway.

Civil engineering work began in 2001, followed by the start of track laying at Hyson Green in October 2001. Test running began in March 2003 on the 'railway' section to Highbury Vale, and over the complete system by the end of August 2003. Training and remedial work followed, and a shadow timetable began early in 2004 with the official opening on 8 March. These pictures follow the process of construction through to completion, a unique record of tramway and light rail building in the twenty-first century.

*All pictures by Martin Cobley*

*Left: Track-laying began at Noel Street on the section where outbound and inbound lines follow parallel streets. First it was necessary to remove the road surface and foundations, and to divert utility services. 2 November 2001.*

*Below left: Rails and reinforcing mesh await track-layers in Noel Street on 9 June 2002, seven months after preparatory work began. The encapsulating material around the rails can be seen: the grooved rail section used in Nottingham has a relatively shallow profile.*

*Below: Nearer to the city centre this is Waverley Street at the future High School stop, on 14 July 2002: here the tracks will be at the edges of the highway.*

Above: After completion of the concrete track foundations on one side of the road rails were delivered to the site ready for fixing. This is Fletchergate near the future Lace Market stop on 3 April 2002.

Top right: Street track was only part of the story: much needed to be done on the railway sections incorporated into NET, and this is the scene on the remaining section of the former GCR viaduct at Station Street on 17 January 2003. The new tram stop will be built immediately above these arches, with a new bridge to Nottingham Railway Station in the distance.

Middle right: Nearer to the city centre the old GCR viaduct adjoining Middle Hill had been removed and a replacement structure was required. On 24 June 2001 a new concrete span is lowered into position, with High Pavement and St Mary's Churches in the background.

Right: Although the Babbington Colliery branch, site of NET's Phoenix Park line, had been in use until 1984, the trackbed required complete reconstruction. This is the scene on 19 March 2002, looking towards the future Cinderhill stop in the far distance.

Left: Along the Robin Hood Line between Wilkinson Street and Bulwell two extra tracks were needed to accommodate NET trams and this is the scene looking towards the future David Lane stop on 11 May 2002. The channel of the River Leen is on the left.

Middle left: North of Bulwell NET required only an additional single line, with passing loops at stops. The Robin Hood Line, too, was singled, but with a lengthy passing loop here at Bestwood Park. This is the view of the future Moor Bridge stop on 11 May 2002, 130 miles from St Pancras as the Midland Railway's old milepost on the right shows! NET's distances on this section are measured in kilometres from Hucknall.

Below left: Work was proceeding on the depot, built on former industrial land at Wilkinson Street. The framework was in position on 22 September 2001.

Below: To reduce noise, vibration, and wear rail joints were welded, and here a small crucible is in use in Noel Street on 11 March 2002.

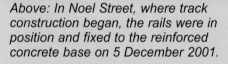

*Above: In Noel Street, where track construction began, the rails were in position and fixed to the reinforced concrete base on 5 December 2001.*

*Top right: The depot was fully functioning on 26 April 2004. The site is large enough to accommodate the increased fleet which will be needed as the system expands.*

*Middle right: The next task was to complete the infill to the railhead, to restore the road surface, and on 27 February 2002 the shuttering was ready for pouring around the rails.*

*Right: Some parts of the railway section also use a concrete track base and here concreting is taking place near David Lane on 9 September 2002.*

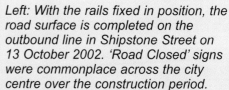

Left: With the rails fixed in position, the road surface is completed on the outbound line in Shipstone Street on 13 October 2002. 'Road Closed' signs were commonplace across the city centre over the construction period.

Middle left: Substantial civil engineering work was needed at several places on the 'railway' sections of the route. This is the new bridge across the River Leen just beyond Highbury Vale on the Phoenix Park branch, seen on 14 February 2002.

Below left: Two years later the bridge was complete, and a tram is crossing it a few weeks after public service began in March 2004.

Below: At the other end of Shipstone Street the future stop is under construction on the left on 9 March 2002.

*Above: The two branches of NET diverge at Highbury Vale, and on 11 September 2003 during the trail running period inbound trams from Hucknall and from Phoenix Park are in place together.*

*Above top: At Highbury Vale track and overhead line were in position by 9 February 2003, ready for the start of test running here four weeks later.*

*Top left: Overhead line installation proceeds on the 'railway' section near Cinderhill on 9 March 2003, using 'road-rail vehicles.*

*Left: After erection engineers check the height of catenary overhead line at Butler's Hill on 14 May 2003.*

*Above: Inbound and outbound lines diverge in Noel Street, with the two lines following 'contra flow' directions so tracks have to cross each other at either end of the section. On 14 April 2002 the diamond crossing was in place, with the outbound line leading from Terrace Street in the foreground en route from Radford Road. This layout imposes a severe speed restriction.*

*Top right: Compared with the great city tramways of a century ago NET is a simple system, but it has its trackwork complications. Just north of The Forest stop the inbound line has a section of interlaced track so that the points leading to the central siding are located away from road traffic in Gregory Boulevard and on straight track. The point blades were being installed on 22 March 2003.*

*Right: There are seven intermediate crossovers on the system, to allow operational flexibility and emergency working. This is one of street track crossovers under construction, at Goldsmith Street near the Royal Centre stop on 4 May 2003.*

*Below: After completion of the road surfaces and addition of road markings the track layout at Noel Street is seen on 16 September 2003. The inbound line on the right has swung out of Terrace Street whilst the outbound line can be seen continuing up Noel Street in the background.*

*Above: A familiar sight in the city centre is the imposing portico of the Theatre Royal at the top of Market Street. On 9 June 2002 track is in position at the top end of the street, only part of which was closed at a time. Track for Nottingham's first generation tramway also used this street.*

*Left: At the outer end of the parallel working section the two single lines meet again at Wilkinson Street, where the trackwork is made more complex by the double turnout leading to the depot. This is the scene looking outwards towards Wilkinson Street stop on 13 July 2003, with the inbound line to Radford Road in the left foreground.*

*Left: Further from the city centre the outbound track was partly complete in Goldsmith Street near Nottingham Trent University on 5 May 2002.*

*Below: On 22 March 2003 track and platforms were in position at Hucknall stop, with the overhead line poles awaiting their wires.*

*Above: Cinderhill stop is attractively - but awkwardly - located in a cutting adjacent to the nineteenth century Cinderhill Road Bridge. Its location requires this sinuous pathway to facilitate disabled access. 7 May 2003.*

*Right: With trackwork in hand, work proceeded on fitting out the stops. The present Station Street terminus is unique in having lift access as well as a bridge to the nearby railway station, and on 16 September 2003 the tower framework was being installed. The truncated end of the viaduct is behind the crane: the planned extension will proceed southwards from here, crossing the railway station to the left of the picture.*

*Right: The inbound line follows one lane of Radford Road on the parallel working section, with a stop on the pavement. On 11 May the stop was almost complete, with the passenger shelter shrouded in protective packing and the passenger information display awaiting installation on the bracket in the foreground. Overhead line will be erected shortly.*

*Below: One of the sharpest curves on the system takes NET from road-side location at Wilkinson Street down to join the Robin Hood line. The ramp can be seen here on 12 January 2003, with track and overhead catenary nearly complete. Trial running would begin two months later.*

*Above:* Testing and training continued for nearly a year after completion of the first section of route in March 2003. During the test period, on 16 September 2003, tram 202 – the first to arrive on 24 September 2002 – glides into the new Phoenix Park business park built on the site of former Babington Colliery.

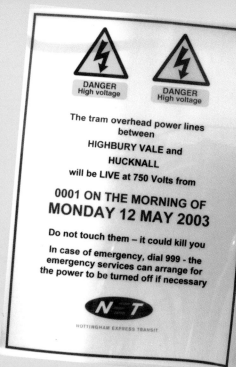

⚠ DANGER High voltage   ⚠ DANGER High voltage

The tram overhead power lines between

**HIGHBURY VALE** and **HUCKNALL**

will be LIVE at 750 Volts from

**0001 ON THE MORNING OF MONDAY 12 MAY 2003**

Do not touch them – it could kill you

In case of emergency, dial 999 - the emergency services can arrange for the power to be turned off if necessary

**NET**
NOTTINGHAM EXPRESS TRANSIT

*Above:* At last! On 12 May 2003 the system went live between Highbury Vale and Hucknall, the section from Wilkinson Street having been energised in March. By the end of August 2003 the system would be complete through to Station Street.

*Left:* On the opening day, 8 March 2004, a tram waits for custom at Hucknall terminus, with the park-and-ride car park on the right and the twin single lines of NET and Robin Hood stretching away southwards. New loading points for the Trent Barton feeder bus service would later be installed adjacent to the tram platform.

*Left:* By 31 March 2004, three weeks after opening, the tramway was established as part of Nottingham's urban scene. Tram 204 crosses the new viaduct and swings from the inbound track to the outbound platform. Three years of construction were over: the new extensions will one day be taking trams further south.

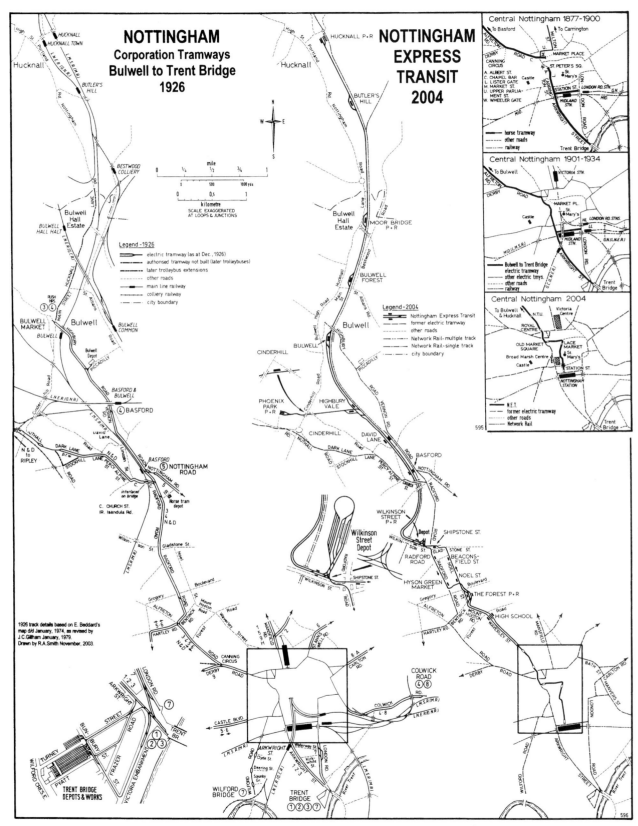

*This map shows the NET track layout in full, and also the relationship with the former Nottingham tramways (Courtesy Tramway Review).*

# Chapter 5 'Surfing the NET': A ride on Line One

## Through the City Centre

Let's try the first line of Nottingham's revived tram system. This consists of a 12.3 km main route to the neighbouring town of Hucknall, and a short 1 km branch from Highbury Vale to a business park and park-and-ride site at Phoenix Park in Nottingham's western suburbs. Line One includes a lengthy street-running section through the city centre, but the line starts on the former route of the Great Central Railway, on a partly-rebuilt viaduct, and the section north of Wilkinson Street consists of new track laid alongside the National Rail Robin Hood line, reopened here in 1993. The subsidiary Phoenix Park branch also runs over a former railway, in this case a Midland Railway mineral line once serving Cinderhill Colliery.

*The present southern terminus at Station Street stands high above ground level on a remnant of the former Great Central Railway viaduct.*

Our journey begins at the smart Station Street terminus, raised high above Station Street itself on a short remaining part of the old GCR viaduct. There is a bridge across the street linking directly to the footbridge crossing National Rail's Nottingham station, thus giving simple access from each platform to the tram terminus. The station itself, although largely rebuilt by the Midland Railway early in the twentieth century, urgently needs rehabilitation, and a project now exists to establish a major inter-modal interchange here, incorporating the extended tramway. Station Street NET stop is more elaborate than others on the present system, with a large covered waiting area on the right hand platform, and lift access from the street. The right hand platform is longer, with room for two trams if required, and there is a scissors crossover just beyond the platform end.

*On the approach to the station from the north a scissors crossover provides maximum operational flexibility. The position-light indicators show the points position. Like other pointwork on segregated sections of the line timber sleepers are used under the crossover.*

The GCR, opened in 1899, once continued over massive viaducts southwards across the Midland Station, and northwards into tunnels under central Nottingham, but as we have seen these north and south sections were disposed of in the 1960s and were mostly no longer available for reuse. Our journey begins over a short section of the surviving railway viaduct as far as the bridge over the Nottingham Canal, whence a new concrete structure extends over Canal Street to a signalled junction with Middle Hill where we merge with other traffic. The portal of the former GCR tunnel used to be visible on our right, near what was once Weekday

*The Nottingham Canal passes beneath Station Street platforms.*

At Middle Hill the tramway leaves the viaduct and merges with road traffic. The original railway route continued to the left. A traction substation is situated below the viaduct.

Climbing steeply up Middle Hill the tram reaches Lace Market stop in an historic area now being rehabilitated. The southbound platform here, on the left, is the only one without a passenger shelter.

Beyond Lace Market the tram enters one of the sharpest curves on the system, turning and descending into Victoria Street.

Victoria Street and The Poultry lead gently down into the Old Market Square. (Courtesy Robert Darlaston)

Old Market Square stop is overlooked by the impressive neo-baroque Council House.
In March 2004, shortly after the system opened, banners on the building's front proudly welcomed the new trams. (Courtesy Robert Darlaston)

Skirting the Market Square the trams climb Beastmarket Hill, site of one of Nottingham's original tram routes. This southbound tram is about to turn into South Parade and the Old Market square stop.

Cross Junction, but in 2007 building work began, covering the short remaining stretch of the GCR formation. We pass on the left the utilitarian back of the large Broad Marsh Shopping Centre, which is shortly to be redeveloped, possibly with an additional tram stop close by. Climbing on street through an area rehabilitated with entertainment venues, bars and restaurants the tram reaches **Lace Market** stop, adjoining a conservation area now regenerated, partly with stylish 'city centre living' apartments.

There follows a very sharp leftward bend into Victoria Street and then a drop down to the traditional centre of Nottingham, the Old Market Square, a large open space completely rebuilt between the wars when the traditional street market was moved elsewhere. A further redesign of the area has been completed recently.

The impressive neo-baroque Council House, designed by Nottingham's distinguished architect T C Howitt and opened in 1929, is on our right as the tram pauses at the **Old Market Square** stop. A transport information office occupies one of the shops on our left, where maps, timetables and other information about bus and tram services in the City are available. We enter now one of the two sections of NET which follow part of the route of the original Nottingham tramway, in this case as far as the next stop.

The tram turns sharply right into Beastmarket Hill and then climbs up steep Market Street with the handsome pillared portico of the nineteenth century Theatre Royal straight ahead. Crossing the controlled junction with Upper Parliament Street, the tram pauses at the **Royal Centre** stop alongside the restored and enlarged theatre, with its auditorium by the celebrated theatre architect of the era, Frank Matcham. The stop also serves the adjoining Royal Concert Hall completed in 1983. A short walk down Upper Parliament Street to our right is Nottingham's premier shopping complex, the Victoria Centre, which occupies the site of the huge Victoria Station closed in 1967. Only the station's fine clock tower and hotel now remain.

Leaving the centre now, the tram line climbs up Goldsmith Street, a secondary main road stretching north-westwards out of the city. Most of the area on both sides of the tramway here is occupied by the

*After climbing steeply up Market Street the outbound tram crosses Lower Parliament Street and passes Nottingham's celebrated Theatre Royal.*
*The original trams crossed this view.*

*Just round the corner from the Theatre Royal is Royal Centre stop, which also serves the Royal Concert Hall and other popular entertainment venues.*

*Royal Centre stop is situated on a short stretch of dedicated roadway reserved for trams. In the autumn of 2004 trams were supporting 'Red Nose Day', a national charity appeal.*

Nottingham High School is served by a curb-side stop in Waverley Street. A driver-training tram pauses on a day typical of the wet summer of 2007.

An outbound tram crosses Forest Road before descending to The Forest. Nottingham's last-built horse tramway crossed here.

Attractive Mount Hooton Road leads down to The Forest stop with its centre reversing siding. The parked van was associated with points maintenance work.

The Forest is the start of the most complex section of track on the present system. Off to the right is one of NET's five park-and-ride sites, and round the corner in the far distance the tracks diverge into parallel single line sections. The elevated position-light indicators show the points positions for the centre siding.

The outbound single line passes up Noel Street before turning sinuously into Gladstone Street and crossing a small park.

Shipstone Street stop is neatly situated alongside a new play area.

City campus of Nottingham's second university, Nottingham Trent, which was formed in 1992 partly out of the well-established Trent Polytechnic. With over 25,000 students, and the tramway skirting the heart of the site, NTU provides a steady flow of traffic at our next stop, **Nottingham Trent University**. Climbing again up tree-fringed Waverley Street, with the Arboretum on one side and the General Cemetery on the other, we come to the next stop near **Nottingham High School**, another leading educational institution dating from 1513 and located here since 1868. The separate Nottingham High School for Girls is also close by.

The line crosses Forest Road, location of the City's last horse tramway line, closed in 1902 and never electrified, and descending now along Mount Hooton Road passes the end of the parkland known as The Forest, site of Nottingham's famous annual Goose Fair which originated perhaps as long ago as the thirteenth century and was controversially moved here from the Market Place in 1928: it is still one of the City's main annual celebratory events. **The Forest** stop has an additional centre reversing road for use on busy occasions. The stop also serves one of NET's five park-and-ride sites on our right. Notice that the inbound track is gauntleted for a distance, to ensure that the points giving southbound access to the centre siding are located away from curves and traffic.

## Two lines through Hyson Green

On leaving The Forest, Line One enters the most complex part of our route. A short distance after crossing Gregory Boulevard, the tram route divides into two in order to negotiate the narrower streets ahead. The outbound track crosses over the inbound track which merges sharply from our left. (This 'contra-flow' arrangement allows inbound trams to run in the direction of road traffic at the side of Radford Road). Outbound we pass up narrow Noel Street, with kerbside local stops at **Noel Street** and **Beaconsfield Street**, before turning sharply left onto a short and sinuous section of new segregated track across a recreation area, and reaching Shipstone Street stop before we rejoin the inwards track. (The attractive little **Shipstone Street** Playground on the left was thoroughly rehabilitated as one of a number of 'collateral' improvements associated with the tramway). These three stops are of course served northbound only. Joining the inward track which

*At the end of Shipstone Street the tram emerges to cross busy Radford Road, once site of another of Nottingham's original tramways.*

*The southbound single line between Wilkinson Street and The Forest runs in the inbound carriageway of Radford Road.*

*The parallel single lines rejoin in Wilkinson Street, where the track layout provides apparent right hand running for a short distance. This outbound tram is passing the triangular junction leading to the depot on the right. In the far distance is Wilkinson Street stop, and to its right can be seen cars parked in another park-and-ride site.*

At Wilkinson Street catenary overhead line begins, and just over the brow of the hill the NET route turns sharply right and descends to join the Robin Hood line.

At Highbury Vale the two branches diverge, with separate island platforms on each line. This is the Phoenix Park branch platform, overlooked by CCTV camera.

At outbound Phoenix Park tram pauses at the Highbury Vale branch platform. Much landscaping work was undertaken to soften the impact of the NET system.

Bulwell is one of the busiest stops on the system, with the popular shopping centre a short distance away and convenient links to bus services and to the Robin Hood line trains alongside. NET is single line between here and Hucknall.

Moor Bridge stop is one of three passing places on the Bulwell to Hucknall single line section. This inbound tram pauses alongside the Robin Hood Line over the fence, and there is a park-and-ride site on the left.

Hucknall terminus has side platforms alongside the convenient interchange with Trent Barton buses.

*Cinderhill stop appears rural but is conveniently situated in a residential area which it serves with minimal interference.*

*Phoenix Park terminus has a central platform and adjoins a park-and-ride site convenient for the M1 Motorway. (Courtesy Robert Darlaston)*

leaves us to our left, we encounter a short section of street running before reaching Wilkinson Street stop on reserved track to the right of the road. Notice that the inbound track actually appears to involve right hand running for a short distance, a location to confuse overseas viewers with carefully-arranged pictures! On our right is the entrance to the system's depot and maintenance complex reached by a double track triangular junction, and there is also another large park-and-ride site.

The inwards track, on leaving Wilkinson Street southwards, turns right and alongside the left-hand kerb of busy Radford Road, with a stop by the pavement. Here is the Hyson Green area of small shops and businesses, and this is the second section of line where NET follows an original tram route. The inbound tram calls next at Hyson Green Market stop on a short reserved section of track, where the line turns sharply to the left into Terrace Street around the back of the shops before crossing over the outward line and reaching The Forest stop on the journey into the City.

## Parallel working with Robin Hood

Resuming our outbound journey from Wilkinson Street stop, the tramway crosses the Robin Hood Line on a bridge before swooping downwards to the right and taking up a route immediately alongside the National Rail tracks. From here as far as Bulwell both NET and NR are double track: some widening of the route was necessary and the rebuilt course of the River Leen can be seen along the route on the left. The tram line is, of course, fully segregated over the remainder of the route, apart from level crossings, and is mainly laid on ballasted concrete block sleepers. Higher speed is possible, and the overhead line equipment changes to catenary suspension at Wilkinson Street to allow for this and for the higher traction currents required. Our next stop, **Basford** consists of neat side platforms with footbridge access, and then at the next stop, **David Lane**, both tram and railway tracks are crossed by busy Lincoln Street, unusually equipped with full barrier protection for the railway and traffic lights for the tramway. Incidentally, on this section the Bulwell Market route of the original Nottingham tramway ran close by, along Vernon Road, until 1934. This area is heavily built up with homes and business premises.

## Phoenix Park branch

At **Highbury Vale** stop the line divides, with separate island platforms on each branch. In this quite rural setting the two lines are separated by an open space, where there is a special visual display unit telling inbound passengers which platform to use for their next tram. To the left runs the short Phoenix Park line, built over the former Babbington and Cinderhill collieries branch, closed to coal traffic in 1983. This section was always single line, and the tramway runs on concrete-based track where it is quite narrowly confined through a picturesque cutting containing single-platform **Cinderhill** stop on the right. This is in the centre of a residential area, and between two original brick-built railway bridges dating from the 1870s. The tram then climbs steeply to a wholly regenerated former colliery site, and runs alongside the new Millennium Way East and across a couple of light-controlled crossings. The branch ends at the island platform **Phoenix Park** stop, adjoining another major park-and-ride site with the trams providing the link to the city centre. The main A610 road leading directly to Junction 26 on the M1 is a short distance away. The old Nottingham Road a little further south was once followed by the former Nottinghamshire and Derbyshire Tramways' route to Ripley, which became a trolleybus service in 1933.

The terminus is 7.6 km from Station Street, and the running time is 25 minutes.

## On to Hucknall

Returning to **Highbury Vale** stop, the Hucknall service continues northwards alongside the Robin Hood Line, with double line extending as far as the island platform at the next stop at **Bulwell**. Network Rail's track singles just before the stop, and there is a one-platform Robin Hood Line station over to the right, slightly relocated from the station's position before 1964. This allows quite easy interchange between National Rail trains coming from Worksop and Mansfield. Both tram and train now pass beneath Highbury Road bridge near the centre of Bulwell, where Nottingham trams once terminated in the Market Place a short distance away to the left. North of here both tram and rail lines are single track, with three NET passing loops and a stretch of Network Rail double line near Bestwood Park.

Each of the following two stops, **Bulwell Forest** and **Moor Bridge**, has a neat island platform reached by a foot crossing, There is a CCTV supervised, barrier-controlled level crossing at Carey Road just south of Bulwell Forest, remotely controlled by the Network Rail signallers. A park-and-ride site adjoins Moor Bridge stop. Nottingham's large Bulwell Hall housing estate lies to the left of the tramway, the terminus of an NCT trolleybus service until 1965.

We are now on the final section. There is a passing loop and island platform at **Butler's Hill**, where there is also another barrier-controlled road crossing. Line One ends at the town of **Hucknall**, in a two platform stub-end terminal bordered on the left by a large car park and on the right by the single platform Robin Hood Line station. Convenient bays for the Trent Barton feeder bus network adjoin the tram platform. The town centre lies only a short distance away, and the railway continues north to Mansfield and Worksop. Hucknall terminus is 12.3 km from Station Street, and the scheduled journey time is 32 minutes.

*It's a short step down the ramp to connecting buses at Hucknall, and to the large park-and-ride site. The town centre is close by.*

*The stylish appearance of the Incentro tram is captured in this view. Notice the 'pod' containing the CCTV camera above the cab window.*

## The trams

One of the most important recent developments in public passenger transport is the move towards easier passenger access to both rail and road vehicles, and this is now enshrined in legislation. NET is the first UK light rail system fully to comply with the current access regulations.

With ADtranz as one of the original partners in the construction and operating consortia, the original intention in Nottingham was to adopt their distinctive 'Eurotram' design introduced in Strasbourg in 1994 and built in Great Britain. However Eurotram's technical capabilities were unsuitable: in particular the door-cycling times were slower because large single-leaf doors were used and the lengthened dwell times would have required additional rolling stock. The Bombardier 'Incentro' (pronounced 'In-chentro') design was chosen instead, Bombardier Transportation having in the meantime absorbed ADtranz. The Incentro design was first chosen for fleet expansion in the French city of Nantes, where 23 longer versions of the type were introduced in 2000-1. Ten further trams of this design were added to the Nantes fleet in 2005, but Bombardier have elected to promote their Flexity design in its place; Nantes Incentro tram number 374 was, however, tested in Berlin in 2005. It is interesting to speculate what design will be chosen to expand the Nottingham fleet when extensions are eventually approved.

The trams were assembled at Bombardier's

*The outermost bogies are powered, and the wheel and motor assemblies are shielded.*

*Interiors are spacious with wide articulations and plenty of room around the doors. Audible and visual announcements are made of approaching stopping places.(Courtesy Robert Darlaston).*

Litchurch Lane works in Derby, with components drawn from the firm's other European plants. Delivery began with car 202 in October 2002, followed by a period of intensive testing as the full fleet was commissioned. The Nottingham trams were the first on a new British tramway to be built in this country, all four other new tramways having imported complete trams from overseas. The fleet is also the largest new complete series of home-built trams delivered to any British undertaking since the Blackpool 'Coronation' cars of 1952-3. The tram numbering (201 to 215) imaginatively follows on from the highest number reached by Nottingham Corporation's original electric trams. Each car has been named after a notable Nottinghamshire citizen.

Nottingham's fifteen Incentro trams are five-module, fully low-floor vehicles, with three trucks, placed under each of the outermost and central modules, with the outer two bogies powered by a separate asynchronous water-cooled traction motor for each wheel, with automatic sanding. Bogie wheelbase is 1.8 m. SAB resilient wheels are fitted, and there is flange lubrication equipment on the centre (unpowered) bogie. Trams are 33 m long and 2.4 m wide, with four double and two single sets of doors on each side. Each has 62 seats (54 fixed, four tip-up, and four perch places). Allowing four standing passengers per square metre, the capacity of each tram is 191 although more can be accommodated in crush conditions. There are two designated wheelchair positions, with adjacent low-level communication modules. All stops are designed for virtually level boarding. Maximum speed is 80 km/h (50 mph) on the former railway sections of route, but trams are limited to a maximum of 48 km/h on street (30 mph). Maximum service acceleration is 1.2 m/s$^2$, with service braking of 1.4 m/s$^2$ and hazard braking of 2.5 m/s$^2$. Brakes are dynamic, friction wheel, and magnetic track. The trams are designed to cater for a maximum gradient of 8.5 per cent (1 in 12) and for curves with a minimum radius of 18 m, both of which are necessary as fitting the line within the existing street pattern involves some steep gradients and sharp bends.

The operator's cabins are fully enclosed but glazed for passenger reassurance, and there is CCTV surveillance of platforms and to give the driver a rear view. This is an innovation in British tramway operation, which had previously relied on mirrors.

*NET is the first UK tramway fully to comply with access regulations: the gap between platform and car floor is exceptionally small.*

*NET uses grooved tramway rail on street sections and ballasted track or concrete-slab-based track on segregated sections. At Middle Hill the tramway leaves the viaduct section from Station Street and merges with the highway alongside Broad Marsh, and the change from flat-bottomed railway track on concrete to tramway rail is clearly visible.*

*Traditional tramway points are used on street sections, manually controlled in the case of emergency crossovers like this one in Beastmarket Hill.*

*Street track is fitted with track drains connected to the public storm water system, but occasionally (as in the exceptional rainfall during 2007) even these cannot cope.*

*Over most of the section to Hucknall flat-bottomed rail is laid on concrete block sleeps held to gauge by tie bars. As can be seen at Bulwell NET stop, track adjacent to platforms is laid in concrete, precisely to maintain clearances needed to secure minimum gaps between platform and tram floor. A Robin Hood Line train is leaving for Nottingham, non-stop.*

*Pointwork on 'railway' sections is laid on timber sleepers, and points are controlled using electro-hydraulic mechanism. This triangular junction is at the entrance to Wilkinson Street depot.*

Internal passenger information systems include both visual and audible announcements of destinations and approaching stops, and the trams are air-conditioned. Livery is dark green, silver and white, giving an elegant and distinctive appearance rather removed from the modish designs seen on some road passenger vehicles, and also echoing the familiar green colour typical of Nottingham's municipal transport since the 1930s. Most trams bear partial or all-over advertising livery.

## Track

Like all existing urban street tramways (old and new) in the British and Irish Isles, NET is a standard gauge (1435 mm) system. On the street sections between Middle Hill and Wilkinson Street NET uses grooved tramway rail of SEI 41GP profile, supplied by Corus, laid on continuous concrete slab with flush street paving to minimise interference with other traffic. To lessen noise and vibration rail joints were welded in situ, and rails are encapsulated to reduce vibration and current leakage. Most of the 'railway' sections use welded flat-bottomed rail of BS 80A profile on ballasted concrete block sleepers with tie bars, although there is some mass concrete track bed adjacent to platforms and at certain locations on the Cinderhill branch. As noted the line is double track as far as Bulwell, apart from the separate parallel street trackage in Noel Street and Radford Road, and is single track on the Phoenix Park branch and the Hucknall line north of Bulwell. Level crossings use either rubber paving or grooved rail in concrete.

Points in grooved track were supplied by Edgar Allen Engineering Ltd, and are equipped with Hanning & Kohl mechanisms, either electro-hydraulic or manual in operation. On the railway sections pointwork was supplied by Corus, and is also equipped with Hanning & Kohl mechanisms. Some turnouts are equipped with heaters, and facing turnouts have proximity switches to detect proper setting.

A programme of rail grinding using modern rail-mounted contractors' equipment is followed when needed to lessen rail corrugation and consequent noise. NET maintains its own 'Unimog' road-rail maintenance vehicle, which can be used in such roles as snow clearance and overhead line maintenance, and there is a range of supporting road vehicles.

For emergency working and to facilitate operational flexibility there are trailing crossovers on the double-track sections at Old Market Square, Royal Centre, Wilkinson Street, Highbury Vale, and Bulwell, and a bi-directional reversing siding at The Forest.

## Stops

The initial system has twenty-three stops, including its three termini. All except Lace Market southbound have shelters, mainly using a consistent and stylish standard 'kit of parts'. High quality structure design and signing contribute to NET's objective of enhancing the quality of the streetscape.

Station Street, the present southern terminus, is the exception to the standard design and has a more extensive covered waiting area on one of the two side platforms, with steps and footbridge connection to the nearby railway station and to Station Street itself, and – uniquely on the present system – lift access from street level. The standard shelters at other stops are to a modular design, mainly glazed for better visibility, with 'perch' seating, and distinctive metal roofs. Stops are denoted by elevated illuminated 'cubes' with the system logo, and have distinctive radiussed name signs. The predominant system colour is dark green.

On the street sections most stops consist simply of raised sections of the adjoining pavements. The tram floor is 350 mm above rail level, giving almost level access, and there is very small lateral gap between floor and platform edge. Stops have passenger call-points monitored from the Control Centre, and also comprehensive travel information displays, and passenger information screens giving expected waiting times. There are emergency alarms and public address systems.

On the segregated section north of David Lane most stops have island platforms, in the case of those north of Bulwell situated at passing loops. Phoenix Park terminus platform is also between the two stub tracks, whilst at Hucknall there are separate side platforms.

## Park-and-ride and feeder buses

NET stands out from other new British light rail systems in the extent of its park-and-ride facilities, as part of the mission to attract drivers out of their cars. Sites are situated adjoining five stops, at The

*Most NET stops have an elegant and consistent 'kit of parts', comprising shelter, name-signs, passenger information displays and help-points, rubbish bins, and CCTV surveillance. All can be seen here at the southbound platform in the Old Market Square.*

*Simpler on-street locations involve a raised section of the adjacent pavement, like this platform at High School northbound, where the stop and shelter are ingeniously contained in the closed end of Gedling Grove.*

*The present southern terminus at Station Street is exceptional and has lift access from street level, a direct footbridge to the railway station, and a large covered waiting area at track level. The short section of original Great Central viaduct leads towards the city centre.*

*At track level Station Street terminus has twin side platforms of which one (on the left) is long enough to accommodate two trams in case of need. The southwards extension will head over the railway station in the distance, with a new interchange complex.*

*By contrast to urban Station Street the single side platform at Cinderhill is reminiscent of a country branch line. An inbound tram approaches from Phoenix Park.*

*In and around Hucknall the major local independent bus operator, Trent Barton, have introduced a new route network linking several districts to the tram and rail stop. A specially-branded Trent Barton 'Optare' single decker connects with a NET tram in the dedicated interchange area at Hucknall station. Real time bus information is available.*

Forest, Wilkinson Street, Phoenix Park, Moor Bridge, and Hucknall. There are in all over 3000 parking spaces, which are free to NET users. Sites are lightly but attractively landscaped and have CCTV surveillance and regular patrols from security staff. The park-and-ride sites are extensively sign-posted from nearby main roads.

Both Nottingham City Transport, a partner in the NET consortium, and the important – and still independent – large local bus operator, Trent Barton, introduced bus route revision to feed NET effectively, and Trent Barton, in particular, devised a new high-frequency local network around Hucknall under the 'Connect' banner, to link outlying estates to the light rail terminus. Joint ticketing arrangements with both operators encourage intermodal travel.

## Power supply and overhead line

The power supply system derives from practice established by experience over a century or more, and whilst making use of state-of-the-art equipment builds on tried and reliable technology. The trams collect current from overhead line equipment energised at 750v dc. (Given the relatively short distances involved, as well as safety considerations applicable to on-street operation, a higher voltage, as now almost universally adopted for railway applications, is not appropriate). The overhead is supplied from six traction sub-stations, situated at Middle Hill, near Station Street (1400 kVA), The Forest (1600 kVA), Wilkinson Street (1400 kVA), Babbington Junction, Highbury Vale (1600 kVA), Moor Bridge (1200 kVA), and Butler's Hill (1100 kVA). All are remotely monitored from the Wilkinson Street control room.

Determined efforts were made to minimise the visual impact of overhead line equipment on NET's on-street sections, in contrast to some other modern installations, and maximum use has been made of suspension from adjoining buildings. This has greatly reduced the 'steel forest' of traction poles in the city centre streets, and provides a best-practice benchmark for future systems. Suspension of the overhead line on the street sections is by simple span wires On the railway section from (and including) Wilkinson Street northwards catenary suspension is used (apart from on the Phoenix Park branch and adjoining some platforms), as speeds

*Passengers arriving at Nottingham railway station are directed straight to the nearby NET trams linking to the City Centre.*

*Name boards are of a distinctive radiussed design.*

*The 'kit of parts' at NET stops always includes a distinctive pole-mounted cube.*

*Full directional information is given to passengers arriving by car, cycle, or on foot.*

*Even litter bins have been specially designed and identified with the system symbol.*

*Access to many NET stations is by foot crossing and national standard warning signs are displayed.*

*Right: Five of Nottingham's seven park-and-ride sites are served by NET, and the system is comprehensively sign-posted. This sign includes the symbol of the Robin Hood Line.*

*The Trent Barton bus feeder network around Hucknall operates under the 'Connect' brand as this stop sign shows.*

*The NET system is supplied with current through six traction substations remotely monitored from the control centre at Wilkinson Street. This is the Moor Bridge substation.*

*On street sections and the Cinderhill branch overhead line equipment is of the simple trolley-wire type supported from tubular traction poles. This is the span wire arrangement near Station Street, with a section insulator and feeder from the nearby Middle Hill substation.*

*On the 'railway' section catenary overhead is mainly used, to allow for higher speeds and to cater for heavier power requirements. The catenary begins at Wilkinson Street stop.*

are generally higher and power requirements correspondingly greater.

Traction poles are uniquely identified by the section code and distance in metres from a datum point at Hucknall. The Cinderhill branch poles are separately identified in a sequence starting from Highbury Vale junction.

## Signalling and communications

Traditionally tramways have operated on 'line of sight' without safety signalling, and this principle prevails in Nottingham. However, on single track sections the exits from passing loops were often governed by simple indicators. Although even in Great Britain there were instances where tramway signals were latterly installed to give a separate phase in road traffic control systems this was exceptional, and it was not until the revival of light rail that the more modern concept of tramway signalling integrated with road traffic lights was adopted. In Nottingham stop/proceed position-light indicators are integrated with traffic signals at intersections on the street sections, and trams are identified using inductive loops. Points positions, for instance at the reversing siding at The Forest and at the termini, are separately indicated.

On the former railway section north of Wilkinson Street the light rail indicators also use LED position-lights rather than colour lights, and there are warning indicators on the single-track Cinderhill branch and between passing loops on the Hucknall line north of Bulwell. Alarm indicators show if a driver enters an occupied section.

Speed limits are indicated by diamond-shaped black-on-white signs as prescribed in the national Traffic Signs Regulations.

## Depot

NET is operated from a depot and control centre built on former industrial land at Wilkinson Street, situated at the northern end of the street section and adjacent to one of the main park-and-ride sites. Stabling is provided for the initial fleet of 15 trams, with a three-track covered depot providing for sanding, for under-car inspection from pits and high-level inspection from gantries, and a jacking road without overhead line leading to a wheel lathe. Adjacent are a four road open-air stabling area and a washing plant.

A battery shunting tractor is provided for internal movements within the complex. A balloon loop is provided beyond the maintenance building to facilitate turning the cars periodically. Space is available on site to accommodate expected increases in the fleet.

## Control Room

As is normal for modern rapid transit systems, a comprehensive integrated control centre is housed in the administrative block at Wilkinson Street. The dominant feature is  bank of twenty-four high definition flat screen monitors receiving feeds from CCTV cameras at stops and elsewhere. The monitors cycle between different cameras, which can also be individually controlled. Camera feeds are recorded in case subsequent action is required. The Duty Manager, with his own VDU console overlooking the CCTV bank, also monitors and controls power supply, including section electrical isolation when needed. Radio contact is maintained with all trams and with other operating personnel.

*Position light indicators on NET advise drivers of the status of track ahead on single-line sections, and show special phases in road traffic signal cycles. At High School the NET indicator is fitted above the road traffic signals.*

## Tickets and fares

In world terms the NET system was unusual in avoiding off-tram ticket sales from machines at stops and by adopting ticketing by on-board customer service staff from the start. After the Second World War most remaining tramway systems in the world moved, for economic reasons, towards a mixture of off-tram ticket sales and sales by drivers working as the sole on-board staff. More recently machines, some of almost baffling complexity, were installed at stops, and most wholly new systems have not involved drivers in ticket sales at all.

Although such procedures may appear to offer financial advantages, experience has shown that anti-social behaviour is hard to prevent and control if drivers are isolated from the passenger areas, especially where very long vehicles are in use. This is turn deterred off-peak riders, especially at night. Ticket machines, which were introduced from the start at the other new British tramways, proved unreliable and prone to destructive vandalism, and both Midland Metro and Sheffield have largely removed them. These and other operators, including some in Europe, have re-introduced tram conductors, or 'customer service assistants', although in contrast to traditional operations these staff are not responsible for stopping or starting procedures.

On-board staff are able to monitor safety procedures, limit vandalism, and ensure to a greater extent than occasional inspections that appropriate fares are paid. However about half of users of NET buy multi-ride or multi-operator tickets in advance from

NET

NOTTINGHAM EXPRESS TRANSIT

Ticket Type:

Ad TramRider

From:

Station Street

Valid as far as:

ALL TRAMS

or

Valid Until:

20MAY07          01:00

Fare Paid

£2.20

736234 0207 12HF 0552 13:41

www.thetram.net

*NET uses the 'Wayfarer' ticket-issuing system*

*Left: All traction poles are uniquely identified with a section code (derived from the stop name) and a distance from datum points at Hucknall and Highbury Grave. This pole is near Bulwell, located 4.570 km from Hucknall.*

*Centre: Speed limits are indicated by diamond-shaped signs.*

*Right: All stopping places are equipped with passenger help points connected directly to the control centre.*

*At Moor Bridge northbound this repeater indicator informs the driver that the subsequent indication at the shunt limit is clear for access to the single line section.*

*These two indicators at the exit from Hucknall show that the points are set for the right hand track, but that the single line section ahead is blocked.*

numerous retail outlets, and there are several different schemes offering through ticketing with both NCT and Trent Barton buses, and National Rail trains.

The on-board staff use battery-powered 'Wayfarer' ticket-issuing machines, which comprise a hand-held computer and input keyboard, designed to be operated by the thumb of the left hand, communicating with a belt-mounted printer unit. Data can be downloaded to the depot computer through an infrared port, automatically providing traffic data and shift totals. Although a little slower than some traditional systems, the Wayfarer offers a far wider range of tickets and data, including the capability to read credit and debit cards and other stored-value smart-card applications when available. Ticket sellers are also located at some busy tram stops in peak periods.

NET operates with a range of flat fares as well as period and multi-trip tickets. In June 2007 a single peak-period one-trip fare cost £2.30, an off-peak fare £1.40, an all-day ticket £2.40, and an all-week ticket £11. In addition there is a wide range of longer period and multi-trip tickets, including special student fares, and combined tickets offering travel by tram and NCT and Trent Barton buses and Central Trains. From March 2007 NET signed up with the 'PayPoint' system, offering a range of discounted prepaid tickets bought through a network of local agents: for example, a seven day tram ticket cost £9.

## Timetables

The working-up period for entirely new transport systems is always difficult and NET wisely decided not to assume that vehicle availability would reach optimum levels from the start. The opening timetable offered five trams an hour in the peak periods to both Phoenix Park and Hucknall, giving ten trams an hour over the main line south of Highbury Vale on Mondays to Fridays. These intervals lengthened slightly over the midday period to four trams an hour over each branch, with three an hour in the early mornings and after about 18.30. A four-an-hour service operated on each branch for most of Saturday and a two-an-hour service on Sunday.

With staff fully experienced, and with vehicle reliability established, the frequency was improved from January 2005 to a six-an-hour service over each branch at peak periods on Monday to Fridays, five trams an hour in the midday period, and also five an hour for most of Saturday. Sunday service was increased from two to three trams an hour. Continuing traffic growth led to a further service enhancement from October 2005. Five to six trams an hour now run on each branch between about 07.15 and 18.30 on Mondays to Fridays, with reduced frequencies in the early mornings and evenings. Six trams an hour run on each branch much of the day on Saturdays and four an hour on Sundays. This frequency is probably the maximum that can be offered with the present fleet, requiring about thirteen trams in service out of the fleet of fifteen. However it is, of course, possible to extend the period of the day in which maximum services operate, for example so as to meet special traffic requirements such as the annual Goose Fair.

On Mondays to Saturdays trams normally operate from Station Street between 06.00 and just after midnight, from Phoenix Park between 05.58 and 23.38, and from Hucknall between 06.02 and 23.35. On Sundays and Public Holidays services start about two hours later and end about an hour earlier. There are short workings to and from Wilkinson Street at the start and end of traffic, and at changeover times in the service frequency.

## Publicity and marketing

NET has been particularly vigorous and effective in promoting the system and in providing user-friendly information about it. The close links with Nottingham City Transport buses has helped to facilitate a range of stylish and colourful printed publicity emphasising the inter-modal aspects of the operation, and NCT's journey planners included tram information. Displays at stops have been particularly effective, in contrast to the situation in some other operations. A comprehensive website www.thetram.net supports printed and displayed publicity. All stops display real time passenger information.

## NOTTINGHAM LIGHT RAIL
## DIAGRAM OF TRACK LAYOUT, WITH LOCATION CODES

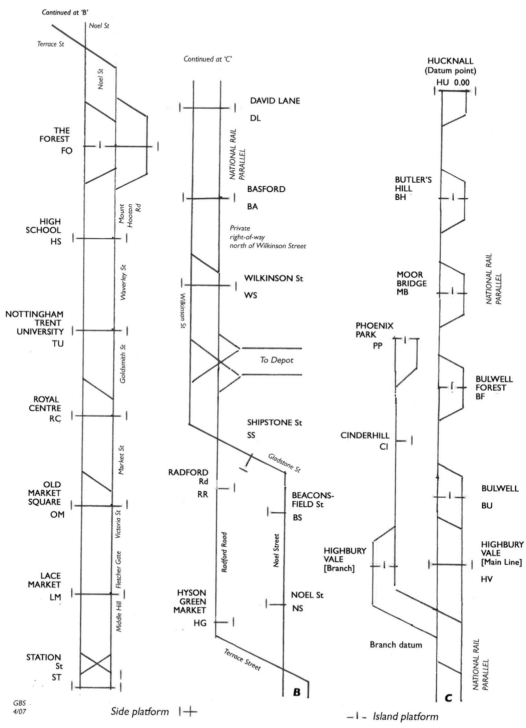

*Continued at 'B'*

Noel St

Terrace St

Noel St

Continued at 'C'

THE FOREST
FO

HIGH SCHOOL
HS

Mount Hooton Rd

Waverley St

NOTTINGHAM TRENT UNIVERSITY
TU

Goldsmith St

ROYAL CENTRE
RC

Market St

OLD MARKET SQUARE
OM

Victoria St

Fletcher Gate

Middle Hill

LACE MARKET
LM

STATION St
ST

GBS
4/07

*Side platform*  |—|

NATIONAL RAIL PARALLEL

DAVID LANE
DL

BASFORD
BA

*Private right-of-way north of Wilkinson Street*

Wilkinson St

WILKINSON St
WS

To Depot

SHIPSTONE St
SS

*Gladstone St*

RADFORD Rd
RR

Radford Road

Noel Street

BEACONS-FIELD St
BS

HIGHBURY VALE
[Branch]

NOEL St
NS

HYSON GREEN MARKET
HG

*Terrace Street*

**B**

HUCKNALL
(Datum point)
HU  0.00

BUTLER'S HILL
BH

MOOR BRIDGE
MB

NATIONAL RAIL PARALLEL

PHOENIX PARK
PP

BULWELL FOREST
BF

CINDERHILL
CI

BULWELL
BU

HIGHBURY VALE
[Main Line]
HV

*Branch datum*

NATIONAL RAIL PARALLEL

**C**

—|— *Island platform*

*Schematic diagram of track layout.*

56

*NET adopted on-board ticket-issuing and inspection from the start: a customer service assistant is seen at work in 2007.*

*Successive editions of NET's timetable show the colourful style adopted. The guide contains a comprehensive map.*

# Chapter 7 The next steps

NET's initial line opened in 2004 was always envisaged as the basis for an eventual network serving more of the Greater Nottingham area.

The consultants' studies which began in 1989 identified fourteen potential route corridors into Nottingham, of which six were found to derive the greatest benefits from introduction of higher-quality public transport. Line One of NET had the best prospects of all and was accordingly given priority. Three of the other corridors extended south of the City, towards West Bridgford, Clifton, and Beeston, and it is the last two of these which were chosen in 2001 for development work aimed at the further expansion of the system. (The Clifton and Wilford districts were not absorbed within the City of Nottingham until 1951, and substantial suburban building, initially of social housing for some 30,000 people, took place south of the A453 road between 1945 and 1969).

The area south of Nottingham presents particular transport problems since the limited number of bridging points across the River Trent concentrate road traffic and therefore make congestion worse. The large planned 'ng2' business and retail park, although north of the Trent, is also expected to be an additional traffic generator, and the possibility of a dedicated NET stop is being used as a significant marketing factor in promoting the park.

The next two planned lines, to Clifton and Chilwell, therefore extend south of the existing Station Street terminus, providing the start of a cross-city network and greatly enlarging the catchment area of the system. As mentioned earlier, the Clifton line takes advantage of some of the surviving routeway of the former Great Central line, left vacant since closure here in July 1967. Having been neglected for over forty years, these former railway lands have developed a distinctive wildlife habitat, and this has been an important consideration in assessing the environmental impact of the extension.

Both the planned lines extend southwards from a rebuilt Station stop, with a new viaduct across the Midland Station which is itself planned for major improvement and rehabilitation, with improved direct access between trams and trains. The two lines then diverge to the south of the railway station, at Meadows Way.

# NOTTINGHAM LIGHT RAIL
## Planned extensions

Routes and stops eventually approved may differ

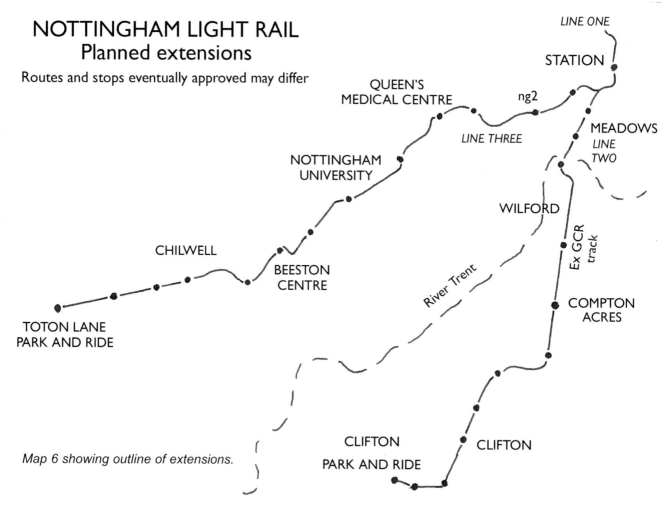

Map 6 showing outline of extensions.

## Line Two: Clifton

Unfortunately, as mentioned, the GCR viaduct and trackbed through the Meadows district as far as the river, which might have been used for the planned Clifton tram route, was completely removed and replaced by housing in the 1970s, and the new line will instead follow a parallel ground-level alignment, partly on reserved track.

Line Two extends through the redeveloped Meadows residential area, across the River Trent on a new bridge adjoining the old Wilford foot crossing, through Wilford village and then onto a 2.5 km section of the old GCR embankment between Coronation Avenue and Clifton Boulevard, with three stops serving the southern end of Wilford, Compton Acres, and the western edge of West Bridgford (the railway embankment forms the eastern boundary of the City of Nottingham on this section). This railway alignment avoids disruptive construction through the built-up areas, but as mentioned has raised vocal conservation concerns.

The line then runs on street through the centre of the Clifton estate, along Southchurch Drive and Farnborough Road, terminating near the southern end of the estate at an important park-and-ride interception site adjoining the main A453 road, which is itself a feeder from Junction 24 on the M1 motorway.

The total length of Line Two is 4.7 miles (7.6 km), with eleven intermediate stops. Almost two-thirds of the route is on segregated track, the remainder shared with other traffic. Journey time from Nottingham city centre is estimated to be about twenty-four minutes.

## Line Three: Beeston and Chilwell

Line Three is the longer and the more complex of the two planned lines, and serves important traffic objectives such as Beeston town centre, the University of Nottingham main campus, and one of the area's principal hospital complexes. NET's plans involve extension from the junction with Line Two south of Nottingham station, westwards through the planned 'ng2' retail park, across the main line railway on a new bridge at Lenton Lane, and then on elevated structure past the Queen's Medical Centre (Nottingham University Hospital). The line then rejoins a street-based reserved alignment past Nottingham University. At the end of University Boulevard begins a complex routing through the Beeston area on a succession of on-street sections involving some property demolition, and with stops serving Middle Street and Beeston town centre.

Passing along Chilwell Road and Castle College, the line then enters a long section of segregated track first along a former watercourse which would be culverted and then on roadside reservation, through the Chilwell district before ending at a further park-and-ride site with some 1,400 spaces at Toton Lane off the A 52, which leads directly to Junction 25 on the M1.

With the existing Phoenix Park terminus on Line One and the proposed Clifton Park and Ride on Line

*Seen across one of the less attractive parts of Nottingham railway station the present end of the NET line is poised to take off southwards.*

Two, all three successive main junctions on the M1 (Junctions 24 to 26) which serve Nottingham will have NET park-and-ride facilities, a clear indication of the utility of light rail in deterring city centre motoring.

The total length of Line Three is 6 miles (9.8 km), with 13 intermediate stops. Over half the route is on segregated track, the remainder shared with other traffic. End-to-end journey time is estimated to be thirty minutes.

About fifteen further trams would be required to operate the two new lines, which would increase the total extent of the network to about 31 route km. with 51 stops. Passenger traffic is estimated roughly to double. Further additional vehicles are also desirable to cater for the continuing build-up of traffic on the original lines.

## Outline Government Approval

With these preliminary route proposals largely resolved, the plans moved a step closer to realization in October 2006 when the then Secretary of State for Transport, Douglas Alexander MP, gave programme entry approval to the project and announced that the Government would in principle authorize expenditure of up to £437m. Three quarters of the total cost is expected to be met through a Private

*Ready to go: NET trams stand at the present terminus.*

Finance Initiative credit, the remainder being split between sources available to the two sponsoring Councils.

The Government's decision allowed the Councils to proceed further with detailed design work, and to apply for statutory powers under the Transport and Works Act.

In making his announcement Douglas Alexander paid tribute to the results of Line One: "The Nottingham tram has been a great success in encouraging people onto public transport. These extensions provide the opportunity to continue this success, and give people in the south of Nottingham quicker, more convenient access to the city centre".

The application for an Order under the Transport and Works Act was approved by Nottinghamshire County Council on 22 February 2007, and by the City Council on 5 March. The full application itself was published on 26 April 2007 and will initially be considered by the Department for Transport. This is, it should be emphasised, a first step in the approval process and much needs to be done before trams run to Clifton and Chilwell. The Department for Transport announced in July 2007 that, as expected, a Public Inquiry was to be held to consider the extension plans. The Inquiry would begin in November 2007 and was expected to last up to six weeks. Once final consent is given, construction of the two lines is likely to take about three years.

Although it is a distant prospect, further possible routes have been identified, eastwards to Sneinton, Colwick, and possibly Gedling; and westwards to Wollaton. The Phoenix Park line could be extended westwards towards Kimberley.

# Chapter 8 The results of NET

In its first two years of operation (2004-5 and 2005-6) NET carried some 8.4 million and 9.7 million passengers respectively, taking the system past its projected targets of 8 million and 9 million journeys. In 2006-7 ridership rose further, to 10.1 million journeys.

In the wider context of public transport development and use, Nottingham has achieved an unusual position in Great Britain outside London in having consistently maintained bus (and now tram) traffic over a number of years. In a comparison between six medium-sized world cities undertaken for the UK Commission for Integrated Transport in 2005, Nottingham was shown to be one of only two which had been able to effect a consistent decline in city centre road traffic. Bus use also grew by nearly 8 per cent over the five years to 2005. This upward trend continued after the opening of NET: in the year ending 31 March 2006 bus patronage grew by a further one per cent, making Nottingham the best performing in this respect amongst the eight large English cities outside London. Public transport use in the 'NET' corridor has grown by up to twenty per cent in peak periods. Surveys show that 94 per cent of tram passengers are satisfied with their service.

High visibility marketing of public transport, inter-modal and inter-operator ticketing incentives, and some traffic restraint have reinforced the provision of high-quality public transport, and the result of these measures, including the light rail project, has been to restrain road traffic growth against the national trend: in 2005 the overall volume had remained stable in Nottingham for six years. Average peak period traffic speeds had also increased slightly, again against the trend. This had been achieved without affecting central Nottingham's continued vitality as a retailing and business centre, a striking reversal of perceptions in the 1960s of what was necessary.

The stability of the local bus operations, and of public transport policies within a broader planning framework, is believed by the City Council to be a main reason for Nottingham's untypical achievements in public transport use, since it has facilitated long-term planning of high quality alternatives to the car.

# The Future for Light Rail in England

Great Britain's sole tramway in 1965 has become six, and we now have as many city systems as we did fifty years ago. Over 130 route km of new tramway have been built, and 112 new trams are in service, carrying over 71 million passengers a year, an impressive level of productivity. Nonetheless amongst light rail promoters there is a palpable sense of disappointment and frustration that further projects have not materialised, not least because of the high costs incurred in bringing abortive proposals to the point of full consideration by Government. In 2000 the Government envisaged up to twenty-five new light rail lines by 2010, but fully worked-up projects for South Hampshire, Leeds, and Liverpool were all subsequently cancelled mainly on grounds of much-increased cost. Another UK project, to reintroduce trams in Edinburgh was, however, approved and funded through the devolved Scottish Parliament. Extensions to some at least of the present English light rail undertakings remain probable, however, and such investment in the improvement of existing transport networks is consistent with the recommendations of the 2006 Eddington Transport Study, where it was argued to offer best value in sustaining economic growth in British cities. This is especially relevant in terms of enlargement of the successful Nottingham system.

Such tentative development of light rail is not unique to Great Britain: plans to reintroduce trams in Denmark and New Zealand have so far come to nothing, and after initial enthusiasm developments in Canada have been slow.

In 2004 the British Government agency responsible for evaluating public expenditure decisions, the National Audit Office, reviewed the outcome of the existing light rail projects, at that time excluding Nottingham, and their conclusions were stark. Some projects had fallen short of their estimated passenger figures, although forecasting is difficult and unforeseen external factors, such as housing demolition, were adverse influences. (Both Manchester and, later, Nottingham Line One have however exceeded their traffic estimates). The statutory procedures were found to be slow and costly, and such related costs as utility diversion high. Above all the lack of an overall transport policy and the lack of integration at local level, prevented light rail from achieving its full potential. These considerations were in striking contrast to the results of light rail development in other developed economies such as France and Germany. The decisive factor influencing government, although it was more attributable to methods of procurement and operation than to the intrinsic characteristics of light rail, was the escalating cost of construction.

For the present the prospects for additional light rail systems in England are uncertain, but the Nottingham installation is acknowledged to be a fine demonstration of the mode's potential, practicality, and achievements.

## About the author

Geoffrey Skelsey has contributed frequently to the LRTA's monthly journal *Tramways and Urban Transit*, and its predecessors, since 1966. After graduating from St Catharine's College, Cambridge, he began his professional career as a legal trainee with the former London Transport Board, and is now a full-time writer and lecturer on the history of technology. His transport articles have appeared recently in *Back Track*, *Tramway Review*, and in the Belgian magazine *L'Etincelle*.

*Author pictured in Brussels: courtesy Yves-Laurent Hansart.*

## Acknowledgements

The author's thanks are especially due to Alec Broers for many years' encouragement in the study of innovative technologies, and for his foreword; to the City of Nottingham Local Studies Library for generous help with access to newspapers and other material; to the North-east Midland Photographic Record, Heanor Library for access to their archive of Nottingham transport illustrations; *www.picturethepast.org.uk*, for permission to use copyright images; and to Cambridge University Library and the City of London Guildhall Library for their matchless reference and research facilities.

Many people have helped me in different ways with information and on visits to Nottingham, including especially Bernard Chatreau (Nantes), John Cadisch, Martin Cobley, Christina Raven Conn, Robert Darlaston, Nigel Friswell, John Haggar, Yves-Laurent Hansart, Howard Johnston, Robin Macdonald, Mike Taplin, Nick Tomlinson, David Walmsley, and Steve Xerri. My apologies to anyone I have overlooked.

The opinions expressed in the book are solely those of the author and not of Nottingham Tram Consortium or Nottingham City Transport Ltd.

## Bibliography

Readers interested in following up in greater detail aspects of the fascinating history of transport in Nottingham will find the following books and journals especially valuable:

John Banks *Nottingham 1* [The bus and tram photographs of G.H.F. Atkins] (Glossop 2002)

John Beckett (ed) *A Centenary History of Nottingham* (Manchester 1997)

Stephen Bennett and others *World Cities Research: Report on Comparable Medium-sized Cities* (Commission for Integrated Transport, 2005)

W.H. Bett and J.C. Gillham *Great British Tramway Networks* (fourth edition, London 1962)

David R.H. Bowler *Nottingham Trolleybuses* (Ferndown, Dorset 2006)

Grant Butterworth *Building on the Success of Nottingham Express Transit Line 1* (Seminar, Edinburgh, December 2006)

Theo Crosby *Architecture: City Sense* (London 1965)

K.C. Edwards *Nottingham and its Region* (British Association for the Advancement of Science, Nottingham 1966)

Mac Hawkins *The Great Central Then and Now* (Newton Abbot 1991)

Health and Safety Laboratory *A Survey of UK Tram and Light Railway Systems Relating to the Wheel/Rail Interface* (Buxton 2006)

D. Kinnear Clark *Tramways Their Construction and Working* (1894, reprinted in facsimile 1992)

Adam Marshall *Getting The Connexions Right* (Institute for Public Policy Research, March 2007)

R. Marshall *A History of Nottingham City Transport 1897-1959* (Nottingham 1960)

National Audit Office [U.K.] *Improving Public Transport in England Through Light Rail* (HMSO, London 2004)

Nicholas Owen *History of the British Trolleybus* (Newton Abbot 1974)0

R.B. Parr *Nottingham's Tramways* (edited by Philip Groves) (Crich 1978)

Kenneth Powell *Nottingham Transformed* (Merrell Publishers, London 2006)

J.H. Price *Nottingham's New Transport Policy* in *Modern Tramway*, May 1974

Brian Richards *New Movement in Cities* (London 1966)

Michael A. Vanns *Nottingham (Rail Centres No 18)* (Shepperton 1993)

*Annual Reports* of Nottingham City Transport Ltd
*Light Rail and Modern Tramway* (now *Tramways and Urban Transit*)
*Modern Railways*
*Traffic Engineering and Control* (especially vol 15, No 4/5, August/September 1973)
*Tramway Review*